Praise for the ...

Wow! What a treasure trove of inspiration.

Zig Ziglar said something at a training conference I attended and it has stuck with me since. "People often say that motivation doesn't last. Well, neither does bathing — that's why we recommend it daily."

This book is a 'how to' for business with more than 70 short interviews of CEOs that capture a huge variety of powerful messages. I am going to read one per day as part of my morning ritual (one of the premises in the book, by the way). That will give me more than 70 days of consistent motivation. Zig Ziglar would love this idea.

Whether you read the whole book in one sitting or use it as a daily motivator, I highly recommend it. The 70+ short stories discuss everything from routines to habits to successes and even failures. You learn something from every single one. Fantastic book. Amazing collection. This would be a great gift for every young entrepreneur!

- Allen Sanders |

Financial Strategist and Founder of Empowerment Concepts

What an inspiring amalgamation of leadership stories, habits and principles. Three themes that really stood out to me amongst the rest were hard-work with a purpose, altruistic teamwork and diversity. All aspiring leaders should put this book on their 'must read' list. The sooner you learn these habits/traits and apply them in your profession and life, the sooner you will achieve success! Thank you to each contributor for sharing your innermost thoughts and experiences.

- David Fuess |
CEO, Catapult Systems

The fact that you're about to add *Supreme Leadership Habits* to your library already says volumes about your level of business acumen. You know that the little things you do every day shape your life, including your career. You know that there are patterns successful people use that you can emulate. You know that success is within reach if only you can implement the thinking and doing of people who already are where you want to be. This is the book you need to read and take action on if you too want to grow a profitable business.

- Ali Razi |
Founder & CEO, Banc Certified Merchant Services

Leaders
Press

Supreme Leadership Habits

70+ Entrepreneurs' Secrets to Growing a Profitable Business

Alinka Rutkowska

www.leaderspress.com

1. Leadership. 2. Business communication. I. Rutkowska, Alinka. II. Title.

ISBN 978-1-943386-34-5 (pbk)
ISBN 978-1-943386-33-8 (ebook)

Library of Congress Control Number: 2018915326

To Dean Jackson, who asked me what the best possible service I could deliver was.
As a result, Leaders Press was born.

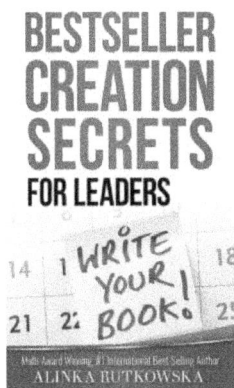

Contents

INTRODUCTION

- Habits
- Secrets
- Philosophies
- Rituals
- Routines

Every successful entrepreneur has developed habits that have played a role in their success, and that's probably why books about daily actions lead the bestseller list.

Think of works such as Stephen Covey's *The 7 Habits of Highly Effective People*, Barbara Stanny's *Secrets of Six-Figure Women* and Gary W. Keller's *The One Thing*.

We answered many questions about what leaders think in our bestseller *Supreme Leadership*.

The journey wasn't over, however; our readers had more questions.

> "How can I be so successful like these leaders?"
>
> "Can I have more detail?"
>
> "How do I get from here to there?"
>
> "What do leaders do?"

This book holds the wisdom of more than 70 CEOs, leaders, founders and presidents of companies with 25 years of experience or more leading in their business.

We wanted to know the details about the habits they formed across the last 25 years that have made them so successful because success certainly doesn't come overnight — and it doesn't come without some intentional choices.

In *Supreme Leadership Habits*, we dive deep into the habits of successful entrepreneurs because habits are what make up our character.

You'll learn the specific actions you can discover and emulate to achieve the results these leaders have achieved.

Even those who thought they didn't have habits realized they did so upon deeper thought during the interviews.

The trends we discovered aligned with daily rituals and ethics ingrained within universal patterns, including:

- childhood formation of entrepreneurship;
- giving versus taking;
- positive habits;
- negative habits;
- morning routine;
- reading and writing.

Are you curious about these features?

Read on.

We've categorized them into short chapters that quickly deliver the most important messages.

See how many of them apply to you.

Even better, see how many you will begin to apply!

PART ONE

CHILDHOOD FORMATION OF ENTREPRENEURSHIP

One thing we were especially curious about was whether or not our entrepreneurs were thinking about the business of making money and about following their passions from an early time in their lives. Had they always been consumed with thoughts of work, money, success and business? Or was it something they chanced upon at some point in life? Was that drive out of necessity or was it innate?

We discovered that for the most part, supreme leaders were at least experimenting in childhood businesses at a younger age, whether it was running a paper route, buying and selling items, or performing chores for family and neighbors.

Does that mean that if you weren't out hustling as a child to earn your spending cash, you might not be an entrepreneur? Certainly not! Read on to discover the different ways several of our leaders got their start and be surprised at the differences.

CHRIS CATRANIS

President, USABROAD, Inc.

www.usabroad.net

My life has been one failure after another, but I've always had fun, and I always made money. I've always lost it too, but I've had fun doing that as well. I don't know if that's considered success or not.

My habits are terrible. I certainly don't have successful habits, but one thing I've done throughout my career is get back up and try again.

My path started when I was 7 years old — at a small barber shop in Lake View, New York, a little suburb outside Buffalo where I grew up. As I waited for my turn in the barber's chair, I was reading a *Hulk* magazine, and in the back, I saw an ad selling a submarine for $15.

This ad listed all the bells and whistles that a boy would think a submarine should have. For example, the ad read, "Imagine going under the water in your submarine and firing torpedoes!" The marketing was clever, and they made it sound like it was real.

Now, I thought $15 was a ton of money, as I was only 7. I got so excited about this submarine that I told all my friends about how we could buy it for $15. They also got excited about it and soon they were begging, "Can we get in on this too?" I'd say, "No problem. What do you want to put in?" They'd offer 17 or 20 cents or their lunch money for the week. In no time at all, I'd collected $5.

Then my father came along and asked what I was doing. He was a technology entrepreneur and an engineer, so he was curious about my budding business. I told him that I was buying a submarine and I showed him the article that I had torn out from the back of the *Hulk* magazine. I explained all the benefits of owning a submarine and how it was going to go through Lake Erie, and I was going to be careful not to go over the falls. I was so excited about it.

My father asked, "Is there any way I can get in on the deal too? How much more money do you need?" When I told him I only had $5, he asked if he could put up the rest.

I said, "Well, sure you can, Dad."

He said, "But I want extra rides."

I said, "I don't know if you can get in the submarine, Dad. I think it might be made for children."

He told me we would work something out, but he was sure he could get in it. "I mean if it's a submarine, they're going to make it big enough for a man, right?"

I agreed with him and took the ten bucks and sent away for the submarine. For the next ten days, I was the most excited guy in the world as I waited for my delivery. Well, ten days came and went. When my submarine finally showed up at the house, it was just a piece of cardboard to set up in my room, and I was expected to imagine I was floating around. I felt like the biggest jackass in the world.

My father came home from work and asked, "What's the matter, son?" I started crying and showed him the cardboard and said, "This is the submarine, Dad."

"Well, that's a disappointment, isn't it?" he said. "What did you learn from that?"

I said, "I learned I'm probably the biggest jerk in the world to think I could get a submarine for $15."

My dad looked at me and said, "No, son. You've learned something much more important. You might not know what it is right now, but you will someday."

I didn't know what he meant by those words, but I did learn decades later. Because with all the ideas I had during my career, I never worried about raising money; I never thought about success. I got excited about my ideas, and I talked about them with other people. When I spoke of them to other people, they got excited too and wanted to be a part of it.

No matter how stupid the idea was.

When people want to put money into my projects, I say, "Look, don't put money into a project of mine unless you're willing to lose it. Because half the time, I lose money. I usually lose it. See, making money and losing money are opposite ends of the same sausage. If you want to be in my business, be prepared to lose. If you're not ready to be prepared to lose, don't put in a dime. Sit on the sidelines and do something safe."

That's how I've lived my life. That's the way I've lived my career, and that's how I run my business. Everybody who is in my business has lost money with me or made money. I lost $60 million of other people's money before I made a dime. I've always paid it back, however.

USAbroad started as an export-management company to sell ball bearings to Scandinavia. I came up with the idea when I did my management thesis for my undergraduate degree at Syracuse University. When I couldn't get a job in international trade after I graduated, I just created my own company.

International trade back then was the sort of position given to retired guys in corporations. They were put in the back corner because nobody took international trade that seriously in America in those days. It wasn't a big thing, except if you were in an oil company or doing foreign exploration or something like that. Most years after the tech boom until now, I've spent my time in the Middle East — mostly in war zones. I work with security companies.

I said recently to a friend that I'm a serial failure. He said, "Oh, no, Chris. You've lived your whole life with these two principles: have fun and make money. That's success. It doesn't matter if you make money or lose money."

If that's the definition of success, I'll take it.

BRIAN LORD

President, Premiere Speakers Bureau
www.premierespeakers.com

I've noticed that our habits tend to be born out of necessity.

My parents got divorced when I was young, so I had a single mom who had four children to raise. We were one of those families that when we'd go to our church, and I'd look in the donation bin, I'd see black-and-white cereal boxes and say, "Mommy, that's just like what we have!" It didn't occur to me that the church pantry was where our food was coming from.

A lot of the things that I had to learn how to do growing up were born out of necessity. For example, we couldn't just go out and buy things. If I wanted something, I had to earn it. As a kid, I became an early bird when I had a paper route. When I started my paper route, I was terrible at waking up quickly. I had to get up at 4 a.m. on Sundays to deliver my papers, but I would be so groggy and stumble around trying to wake up. Most of what we owned were hand-me-downs, so my alarm wasn't an electric one; it was one of those big, round clocks with bells on top that we'd been given by my grandparents — and it was deafening. We had thin walls, and my brothers were on the other side of my wall, and my mom was across the hall.

We had small rooms, and my twin bed took up most of the room. We bolted a frame to the ceiling, so my bed was about six feet off the floor. I would put the alarm clock on the floor to train myself to wake up quickly. As soon as I heard the bells, I would force myself to roll out of bed and fall and land on all fours on the floor to turn the alarm off as quickly as possible. That forced me to wake up and helped me get into that habit of being able to get started as soon as I opened my eyes. It took me about two seconds because there's no option but to wake up if falling six feet out of bed to hit the alarm. I decided I had to learn how to do that if I was going to accomplish what I needed to do. I didn't want to waste time, so that's how I got started being an early bird as an elementary school student, getting up early to deliver papers.

I'm married now, so having a loud alarm six feet below the bed wouldn't go over well with my wife. She's from southern California, and we joke that she's still on Pacific Time. The joke is that I have this whole other life before everyone else wakes up. We adopted twins last year, and I'd find myself up at 4 a.m., and since I couldn't get back to sleep, I'd run. Eventually, I ended up doing a marathon. Even before then, however, I'd usually swim, bike, or run.

It's a habit of mine to wake up — and because it's an easy way to think, I don't listen to music. One of the patterns that I've always found helpful is thinking about things first instead of reacting. Whether it's work or being a parent or being a coach, if you want to do it better, you have to think about it. Many times, we react, or we spend a minute thinking about something instead of saying, "Okay, I'm going to run for an hour, and that gives me time to think about whatever the issue is."

It's always been helpful for me to go out and run under the stars and be able to think and be alone. It's healthy too. Having that extra time alone has always been great. It's also a good time to get better if I want to improve certain things. My early morning habits have been instrumental in my success. Many times, I don't feel like doing something because maybe I'm not in the mood for it; however, having particular habits ingrained for years and years has helped me get up and make it happen.

Another thing that I learned as a child was to engage in constant learning and not to be afraid of knowledge. I had a couple of advantages. My older sister wanted to be a teacher. She is five years older than me, so when she'd get home from school, and before I had even started preschool, she would teach me whatever she was learning because she wanted to be a teacher and I was her guinea pig.

Before I ever got to school, I could read and I could add, subtract, and multiply. The other children were learning how to count to ten or learning what the letters were. That was always a big advantage for me, not because I was particularly smart, but because my sister forced me to learn all this stuff at an early age.

Even though we couldn't afford cable, somehow my mom was able to get her hands on a set of encyclopedias. So I would just read through encyclopedias. As a first or second grader, that opened things up for me. I could talk to adults. Moreover, many times, I would know more about things than anyone else. That was because I didn't have anything else to do, so I would read these encyclopedias. It opened up my mind to different people. I've found that because of that I've always been fascinated by people who aren't like me; people from other countries or different backgrounds. I've always sought out people who aren't like me.

My grandma got me started on reading a particular type of book in second grade, and she offered me $2 for every classic or Newbery Award winner I read. I wanted to get a video game system that was 50 bucks, so I did the math. "Okay, 25 books, 50 dollars — I've got my game system." What ended up happening, however, was that I kept spending money on baseball cards and candy, like any 8-year-old would. So I had to keep learning and learning and keep reading and reading. As a little kid, I ended up reading hundreds of books just trying to buy that game system, and I never actually did end up buying it. I just kept on reading.

Born from my necessity are my habits of getting up early and aggressively going after knowledge. We shouldn't be intimidated by that. There's so much out there to learn. Many people spend all their time thinking about what they don't have or what they can't get, and they miss so much stuff that they already have.

JOHN KULCZUGA

Founder and CEO, Ultimate Machining and Engineering, Inc.

www.ultusa.com

The work ethic I learned from home and the importance of seeing that hard work and how my parents took care of the family of children and provided guidance was helpful later on in my life.

I was born in Ostrowiec Swietokrzyski, Poland. My father was an electrician and my mother took care of my two older brothers and me. The five of us lived in Poland under the communist government in a one-room apartment. For a few years, we didn't have money. I remember getting an orange for Christmas, and that was a treat at that time. It didn't bother us back then because we didn't care about the material stuff. We were happy running down the streets and being friends; that's what counted.

I grew up in a rough environment because of the streets. Not many people there had promising lives. Half of the children were uneducated, and their parents were drunks or in jail, so just a few of the families were strong. The domestic environment is what makes sure the children are not being wasted. So I was fighting for my position on the street, and then having two older brothers was also challenging, so I had to fight from my early years. After going to school, I was active in all kinds of sport, and I would say that doing sport developed the competitive edge and trained me to work to achieve. I would say this was helpful later in developing the right work ethic and has been the most important.

I can't rely on somebody to provide and supply something for me. If I want something, I have to do it myself. I can't wait for somebody else to do that for me. That was my approach. I was hurting all my life; I didn't expect anybody to know to help me. That's because if I didn't have it, it didn't mean I didn't want to have it — it was up to me to do it.

I participated in all kinds of student organizations. In college, with a couple of friends, we created a photographic studio to make a living. We made pictures of families and social events. When a Polish cardinal was elected to be the Pope, we practically worked 24 hours a day to make pictures of him. That's how we provided for our family in spite of the meaningless miserable salary I was making at the time.

I was always curious about how things work. I'm a tinkerer, and that's what I was doing all the time in my childhood; trying to figure out how things work, such as a bicycle or a motorcycle. Whatever equipment I could get my hands on, I took it apart to understand. It was the same later on when I encountered some other problems. It was the happy time I developed in childhood, and I was still doing the same in my adult business life.

I was a good student and worked hard at school and eventually got a master's degree in science at Warsaw University of Technology. I met my wife there. We got married, and had a little girl, and that was in 1980-1981 when the Solidarity movement was under way. This was the time when the government was pushing confrontation with Solidarity to try to crack the movement.

I knew that something had to happen. My income was 2,000 zlotys back then, and we paid around 1,700 to rent our apartment, leaving us 300 for everything else. I had to do other things to make ends meet. At some point, we decided to try our luck outside of Poland as there was no future there for us.

I bought an old car and packed it. We took our 1-year-old daughter and drove through Czechoslovakia to Austria. We managed to cross two borders, and we made it to Austria, and that was a stroke of luck. Getting the proper documents for the family was almost impossible back then, and we were lucky not to run into trouble.

We got to Austria, went to the refugee camp, surrendered our passports, and became refugees. We stayed for one year in Austria, and they were able to get the papers granted, and the green cards for America, and we started new lives in America.

I was 32 when we arrived. I worked for different companies before starting work in my profession of manufacturing and engineering. I worked during the day and went to school in the evening to learn English because back in Poland, I'd learned German. In 1994, having worked for several years for others, I decided to try my hand at the American Dream.

I started Ultimate Machining and Engineering with another Polish guy. There were only two of us, and two machines, a lot of hustle, a lot of energy and not much else. We opened the business, and we managed to buy the first equipment and get new customers. After six months, we were able to get into business with Caterpillar, which is the world's biggest manufacturer of heavy equipment. Caterpillar was a company which enabled us to grow and develop the company, and to learn skills and techniques.

After three years, we moved to a bigger facility to be closer to our biggest customer. We were going through ups and downs like the market, and the economy was going through the cycles, so we were following the economic cycles as well. At some point, we had more than 60 people in the company. In 2003, a huge recession hit, and we had to scale down to 12 people. We survived, though, and bounced back, and now we have 42 people and we're growing again.

The family environment taught me how to treat the family and other people well. This is important, and I'm trying to put aside my business life and my personal life. At home, we might have some arguments with our family members, but at work, I don't believe I have ever raised my voice at anybody who worked for my company.

We treat people as a whole and not just like a cog in a machine. This is a part of why people stay with us; they know that we're not just using their skills before then getting rid of them. We're trying to work with our people all the time. We work with our people and they stay with us.

ITTAI BAREKET
CEO, Netformx
www.netformx.com

I believe that if I want something, I give it my best shot and it is going to pan out.

As a child, I was always a risk taker, and also curious and creative. I think those mindsets helped me find opportunities. For example, I grew up in Israel, and in the summer, we had many watermelons. I noticed that everybody was throwing the seeds away. I thought to myself, "Wait a minute. Why don't I start something in my neighborhood with those seeds?" I started collecting all of the watermelon seeds as they taste good and are just as healthy as sunflower seeds. I dried them out and then roasted them. Then I started selling them, just like sunflower seeds. That was my little business.

I looked around me and saw the opportunity to think about the materials and that something could be done there. I believed that the seeds were going to get consumed. I didn't do much market research or market study. I figured that people consume food, so someone was going to like the seeds. I learned to work with my environment to find not solutions to problems necessarily, but creative ideas.

Another example of childhood entrepreneurship was when I was around 12. I had a sister who was ten years younger than me. We slept in the same room, so I took care of her when she was an infant to a certain degree. My parents didn't bother to send us to summer camps or anything, so one summer I decided to start my own babysitting business. I put leaflets together, saying that I could take the children to the park. There was one family who entrusted their 3-year-old to me. They were looking for solutions for him because they couldn't get him into a camp, and they needed four hours a day for a break. They said they would love for me to take their child to the park.

I had that feeling again that there was a need. I didn't know if people were going to trust me or not, because I was only 12. I figured, however, that I would give it a shot, and I felt confident that I could do it. I gave it my best sales pitch and that family was very happy. I babysat all summer long, and at one point, I had two children to watch who were more or less the same age. I took them to the park and had fun with them and got paid.

Self-confidence can play both ways. I can be confident, and I can make it happen, and I can do it. Sometimes, however, trusting my gut, and believing I can do it, has backfired and turned out not to be successful. That happened in childhood as well.

One of my business ideas that didn't materialize was my decision to deliver milk and bagels in the neighborhood. I was confident that I could do it, but eventually, I ended up having few customers and a bigger investment needed to support them. I had to pull the plug on that business because it didn't work out. My self-confidence versus the market research and analyzing everything ahead of time sometimes works against me.

My parents tell stories about me from before the watermelon-seed business that I don't necessarily remember. My mom's early story was when I was 5 or 6 and was into trading cards.

My mom said to me, "You've had this card for a while. But you're not trading it. So why are you holding onto it? You don't seem to like it."

I said, "Oh, this card has a lot of value. Everybody wants it. I'm just waiting for a price that's high enough; waiting to see how many other cards people are willing to give me before I give this one out. Because I don't want it, but I think I can get more for it."

From my entrepreneurial attempts as a child, I learned and then implemented lessons in my real-life business around persistence, keeping on track, commitment and hard work. The watermelon-seed business was a great example because it was a long process for a 12-year-old to go through. I came up with the idea. I had to collect the seeds, then dry them, put them in a pan in the oven to roast them, add some salt, then package them in paper bags, and go out to sell them.

Throughout that process, there was much commitment to the end product. The journey and the process could be a long one as I had to have that commitment to reach the end goal, and make sure I got there. That stood out for me when I looked at some other peers and saw that when something got hard, many times they gave up and moved on.

I don't. If I decide to do something, then I'm going to be persistent. Moreover, I'll keep on track, even when it's hard. Why? Because I decided I want to do it, and there was a decision and end goal in mind when I made that decision. So I want to make sure I follow it through.

COURTNEY McGEE

Owner, Event Logistics, Inc.

www.eventlogistics.com

I have never considered myself a woman in business; I'm just in business.

Event Logistics is based in Nashville, Tennessee but we travel on a global basis with our clients. We plan strategic meetings, with management for corporate clients and large associations, and we produce events. My husband and I started Event Logistics in 1994, and we're celebrating 25 years next year.

When we started Event Logistics, we decided not to be a woman-owned business, and it has never hurt us. I'm more the visible front person, but we are a company doing high-end, critical programs. If someone thinks about the fact that I'm a woman first versus a business person, it might hold us back.

My habits have played a significant role in my success. A lot of the things that have made me successful at Event Logistics carried over from my childhood. First, I believe it's because my parents were older. My mother was 38 when she had me, so my parents were always my parents — they were never my friends. My mother is 98 now, and if she called me today and asked me to do something, then I would get right up and do it.

My mom was to some extent a 'your father knows best' mom, like Donna Reed. I grew up having my dad working while my mom stayed at home and took care of us. They always attended every single thing that we ever did. We ate dinner at the same time every night. We had to do our homework. It was a very structured life. I didn't know it at the time, but looking back, I think that those things were instilled in my sister and me and helped make us who we are.

I modeled at Rich's department store in Atlanta from the time I was 3 years old until I was 21. We were paid in gift certificates, so I've always worked. My mom made two statements that have stuck with me my whole life, and I know this is from childhood. She used to say, "To have friends, you have to be a friend." That is so true. It takes work, and it takes an effort to build relationships.

The other thing she said was "Can't never could." If I think I can't do something, I'm never going to be able to do it. Those two sayings have always stuck with me. I've got to get up, I've got to go out, and I've got to make it happen. Nobody's going to give it to me or do it for me.

I'm a voracious reader, but I wouldn't say I liked reading until I was in the fourth grade. My mother marched me into the library and introduced me to Beverly Cleary's books, and I realized that I could get a certificate if I read five of them. I wanted the certificate more than I wanted to read — that probably says a lot about me. I read the five books, and I got the certificate, and I've never looked back. I read every day of my life.

I went to the University of Georgia and majored in home economics and journalism. I got married, and then my husband was transferred to Chicago. With those two degrees, I thought it would be natural to go to one of the larger companies and get a job in journalism. It wasn't quite that easy.

As a 21-year-old woman right out of college, I thought I could go to any large company and get a job. It was a catch-22; I needed the experience to gain experience. Even though I grew up in Atlanta, I always felt like I was a big fish in a small pond in Chicago. So that threw some ice water on me.

My first job, ironically enough, came from reading the want ads in the paper to learn about a company that planned programs for convention groups coming to Chicago. So I called and I think just with the sheer force of personality over the phone, I was able to land myself an interview. I went in and thought it was a fascinating company. They called themselves a ground operator, which now is called a destination management company. It's a local company that plans programs for convention groups that come to specific cities.

I was hired on the spot and started the next week and have been in the industry ever since. It was just perfect for me. You can go to college now and get a degree in the hospitality industry, but that didn't exist back in the late 1970s when I was coming up.

The lady who owned that business planned all of the tours for Chicago's Merchandise Mart. Anyone who needed to schedule a group tour — even all of our competitors — had to call to make reservations, and it was initially my job to talk to those folks. I developed an excellent over-the-phone relationship with one of our competitors. One time, she asked me if I knew anyone who might be interested in a sales position.

I was such a good coordinator, but they weren't going to let me do anything different for about two or three more years, so I told her I thought I had somebody who was interested. At lunch, I went down the street, found a payphone, called her and told her I had somebody and that the somebody was me. She hired me, and I worked my way up through the ranks.

It was a fascinating job. On the other hand, all that experience I gained over the years made me start talking about how I wanted to start my own business. I didn't have a plan — that was stupid when I look back from my wise old age now. At the time, my husband Greg was getting disenchanted with the insurance agency, so we started talking about starting a business.

We looked into different things we were interested in. For example, we went to Rochester, New York to talk to a company that had one of the largest barter companies in the country. On the way home, Greg asked, "You like what you do, don't you?" I must have talked about it a lot in that meeting, so I said, "I love it." He said, "Well, do you think you could make as much money for us as you have for these other people?" Hindsight's 20/20, isn't it? I said arrogantly, "Yes, I can do that!"

And that was that. I got up the next morning and went to work on July 3, 1994. I came home that day, and my husband said, "You have to go in and resign tomorrow because I've incorporated a business." He could've knocked me over with a feather! He said, "Well, you've always talked about a meetings-and-events business, so that's what we're going to do."

I said, "Oh my, Greg! What are you talking about? We've gotta come up with a name."

He said, "Well, I've already named it Event Logistics." He was in the transportation insurance business, so he picked the word logistics. Here we are 25 years later, and it's the perfect word for what we do. My husband likes to tell everybody that he pushed me off a cliff and he did. I would've done it on my own — just not as soon because although I had the confidence, I didn't have the knowledge. Our two core skill sets go together to make it successful.

You know, the toughest children go barefoot because "can't never could".

PIYUSH PATEL

CEO, Accelerating Digital

www.acceleratingdigital.com

Probably the first thing that kept me going all these years is that mindset that I had to earn and create versus expecting something to be given to me.

My most positive habit is that I spend much time re-educating myself. I enjoy ongoing education and am always reading, learning, and trying new things above and beyond what's necessary to accomplish a goal. If I had to pick one habit, that would probably be the one that has enabled me to keep striving from childhood until now. I've been able to achieve continually by re-educating myself and always looking to learn new things.

This habit of self-education and improvement was probably cultivated during my childhood, as I grew up with modest means. My parents owned a hotel, and as this was a family-owned business, every one of us worked. As children, we knew that when we arrived home from school, we'd have to clean out the parking lot or prepare rooms. Say the maids didn't come on a particular day, we had to do their job, and we grew up ready to take care of what needed to be done, even as children.

My first job, like many other young boys of my era, was to take on a paper route. I did not do it alone as my mom and my sister both helped me. My mom woke early in the morning to help me fold the papers, and then my sister would help me load them. In my first entrepreneurial venture, I was able to buy a bike with my earnings (although my dad loaned me the money to get the bike first so that I could earn with it). I made money after a certain point and paid my dad back in full.

Many people may not have had the help I did. I can't say that I would have been able to handle my paper route all by myself if my mom didn't get up at 5 in the morning to help me fold papers before school. I probably wouldn't have been able to do it. Having that family support and encouragement was a big factor in my early success. Having that help made a big difference.

As I continued down the path, I had other jobs including checking tickets at a movie theater and washing dishes at the grocery store's bakery department. Even when working for others, I always sought to make my position more productive. I looked for ways to improve upon my duties. I wanted to be able to achieve more. I had, therefore, some hints of entrepreneurship in my nature from the beginning.

The one thing, however, that I was never able to do — because I grew up with modest means with my parents — was to take significant risks. Today, you see many young people graduate from high school or college and make the decision not to pursue employment. Instead, they decide to try their hands at entrepreneurship at a very early age, such as building an app. They feel free to allow themselves to fail.

I never got that exposure as I never wanted to fail. I wouldn't have been comfortable doing so. Our family hotel business failed. We lost the hotel as it didn't make enough money. Understandably, this put a dampener on my wanting to take ultimate risks. Instead, having a job, improving on that job, and increasing productivity was the benefit of me having the experiences I did.

Now, I'm financially secure, and I can take a risk. Many people don't get that opportunity early on. Maybe they don't grow up with the idea that taking a chance is okay because in the U.S. more of the culture is for us all to have steady jobs, grow our careers, increase our incomes, and grow our households. When I was growing up, that was more the thinking than what I see today, which is ease in taking significant risks and starting a business.

In school, I learned the compliance to do an assignment, get a good grade, and accomplish what I'd been told to do, rather than go for the risky entrepreneurial path. I wasn't taught to take risks when I was young, so it took me a long time to start Accelerating Digital and go off on my own and leave the corporate track.

Millennials are taking on much more risk than I would have been comfortable doing. They're doing it in spades today. Without the proper background and education, they can still do it because they don't have that fear of failure. They know they can always move back into their parents' basement. We're at a time now where people are getting more of the exposure that I never had, such as not being afraid to fail, but not enough of what I did get, which was training and planning for success.

TAMI O'CONNOR

President, Educational Innovations

www.teachersource.com

I was a bit of a daydreamer when I was young.

I've always been one of those people who has worked hard. When I was much younger, any opportunity there was to work, sell something, or be a part of a group, I did it. For example, when I was 8 or 9, my mother would drop me off at the local swim club, and leave me there while she and my dad went to work. They would pack me with a sandwich, and in the middle of the day, after I had eaten my lunch, I would go to the snack bar.

I didn't have any money, but I worked out a deal with the owner of the snack bar. It was a large, lodge type of building, so I would offer to sweep the floor in return for a box of Cracker Jacks. At about 2 every day I would show up and sweep their floor, and it was the best-swept floor that they had. I'd get my box of Cracker Jacks, and I'd be happy as pie. I think it was a win-win. Instead of them paying somebody minimum wage to take the half hour or 45 minutes to sweep the floor and move all the chairs, it was worth it to them to trade a box of Cracker Jacks.

I was an only child and grew up mostly without a father, so I would mow lawns in the neighborhood, and stack firewood, even though those were not traditional jobs for girls to do. I did it, and I enjoyed the jobs and got extra spending money. I always liked to feel independent, and that was a good thing.

I grew up in the 1970s, and for part of my formal schooling, I was in a junior high school with open classrooms. From seventh grade until ninth grade, we had partitions between the classrooms. Because I have focusing issues, I would sit in my class, but you couldn't even call it a classroom because the partition was only 4 ft. high. It was about a foot off the ground and had wheels on it, and I would pay more attention to what was going on in the other classrooms alongside me, or whatever was out the window, than I did to whatever my teacher was saying.

There is no doubt in my mind that I have attention-deficit issues, so to focus on the things that I wanted to focus on is relatively easy, but focusing on things that I'm less interested in is difficult for me. I feel like I lost three years of my education in this experimental school setting. Many children have the issue of trying to stay focused, and that just made it so much harder for them. I've always been relatively disciplined about the things that I care about, and fairly undisciplined about the things that I cared less about, or the things that my parents cared more about.

That part wasn't easy. I'm a list maker, so I make a lot of lists. When the list is made, I cross things off, and when I get to a point where I've crossed off maybe a third, I make a new list, and I transfer those things over onto the list. One of the things that I learned in recent years is eating the frog.

Every morning, I think, "So, what's my frog today?" That's generally what I do first because when you finish the one thing that you are dreading at the beginning of the day, the rest of the day becomes a lot easier. That doesn't mean that I don't procrastinate and put things off that I don't want to do; however, I do know that the frog has to get eaten, so that's the first thing I do.

DAVID BROWER

Founder and President, Astro Technology

www.astrotechnology.com

I don't think I was a lot different as a child from what I am now. I stuck with things.

I was entrepreneurial right from the time I was a young boy. I can still remember how when I was 8 or 9 years old, I started my first business to make money so I could buy a baseball glove. My parents didn't have a whole lot of money, but even if they did, I think that I was a self-sufficient, thinking kid.

I cut a lot of grass for a lot of the neighbors. There were many fishermen in the area in which I grew up, so I'd catch nightcrawlers or worms and sell them to the fishermen in the morning. I had a good client base as I did that from the time I was 9.

In high school, most of my time was taken up by sport. I played football, basketball and baseball and continued doing so into my college years. I've always, though, had some business in mind. In fact, I don't ever remember a time when I didn't have some entrepreneurial thing going on.

When I was in college, I did auto body and fender work, for example, and painting and things of that nature to make money. I did that for as long as I can remember. I've never thought differently. I worked for a few years for big industrial corporations in the fabrication and development of rocket motors.

I liked that a lot but my heart was not in big business; it was always in small entrepreneurial pursuits. I want to be able to make quick decisions. Moreover, I don't work well in bureaucratic systems where decisions take forever and must be approved by a committee. I prefer not to work in that type of environment.

Some of the things that have made me a success can also work in the opposite direction. What I mean by that is when we have perseverance, sometimes it's difficult to know when to give up on something because it's not going to go where we want it to go. Perseverance has also to be moderated by sound judgment. Good judgment comes into play even though we have very high confidence in our abilities and very high confidence in the way forward. Sometimes we have to let things go; we have to make those decisions.

The other thing that can be a deterrent with entrepreneurs and people who think the way I do is they sometimes get a little bit too broad and not focused enough on where the dollars will be the best. It's always fun to run out to the lab and do all those wild things. I know I love doing that. Sometimes, however, it's not the best thing because there's not going to be profit potential in some of the things that are fun to do.

I need to be able to look at it objectively and let go of those things that aren't going to offer the reward at the end. For me, that's a challenge. I continually have to moderate myself to ensure that I'm not going down a road that's going to distract me, or it's going to dilute me from the real scope of what the business is.

Specific characteristics that I embody have lent themselves to the success that we've been able to have; things such as perseverance. I've always found it hard to let go; I don't give up easily. Moreover, I've found that in the business world, no matter what I'm doing or what the field is, there are going to be events that happen that have the potential to knock me out of my saddle. I've got to be able to overcome those hard knocks, such as cash flow in a business. Or the technical abilities aren't quite there. Or the schedule is wrong. Or money runs out. Many things can plague a business.

Working in a small business, I've got to be able to withstand those hard hits that are going to come because they certainly will happen. I have to be able to resist those hits and still be the butcher, the baker and the candlestick maker. I've got to be able to do many things. Some of them I may not be as good at as someone else, but I may not have the resources to bring that expertise on board. It can be a real juggling act to keep things balanced, and I must have a tremendous amount of perseverance to survive in the long run.

The tough times can even make you stronger. I may have made it, but it would have been not as fun without people that I enjoyed being around. I view that same thing with the people that I've worked with too. I've made some lifetime friends that I've associated with in our business. I simply like the people, and enjoy some very good working relationships.

That's another essential thing. It's very much about the business relationships that I have and the personal relationships. That's as important, or more important, than the amount of money that I extract out of my business. The business is going to do fine money-wise if it's going to be a success. Those relationships, however, are really the things that make it enjoyable.

I've had some tough times, and I look back with fondness on those times. I've worked with my wife and she has supported me in all of these crazy business ventures. It's her call sometimes. She has been very supportive, and she's not entrepreneurial, so she keeps me in line with the reality of how the cash flow works so I don't get too far out of town with it. That's an important point. This business is jointly owned and run between us. Moreover, we've just celebrated our 40th wedding anniversary. I keep track; we've been married 14,675 days and each day has been better than the last. We've had 520 full moons in that time.

Another thing that's important is that I must consider the vision I have and be confident in it. If I don't have that confidence in my vision, that'll come right back into the perseverance issue, and if I don't have the confidence, I'm not going to be able to keep going. There will be people who will challenge my vision. They may know some things but not a lot. If I believe that I've got the right approach, I stick with it. I trust my intuition and the vision that I have.

PART TWO

GIVING VERSUS TAKING

It's often been said that leaders are successful in business mainly due to the relationships they cultivate. Certainly, every entrepreneur has heard that before. We were confident that our supreme leaders would be able to expand upon how they were successful due to their relationships with others.

By definition, business is financially successful if you make more than you spend. We were curious how this way of thinking was extended to the people around entrepreneurs. The number of times our leaders attributed their success to others was impressive. It's true that you can give more than you take and still make a success of it.

Some leaders give to the customers. Sometimes leaders give extensively to their team. Others volunteer in their communities to give back. No matter how our leaders choose to give, it's clear that giving versus taking is a crucial habit of our supreme leaders.

BOB ROTH

Founder and Managing Partner, Cypress Home Care

cypresshomecare.com

It's not so much that it's important that the people in my team are my friends, but for me to respect them and know as much as I can about them so I can make sure that I'm setting them up for success. If there's something that's going on in their lives, I can help them like I help my clients navigate to a solution.

We're an in-home personal care provider in our 25th year of operation. We cover Maricopa County, which has a total area of 9,224 square miles with about 950,000 people who are 65 and older. I got into this business because on January 2, 1985, I became an accidental caregiver. I say accidental, because it wasn't part of the plan.

I was 22 years old, and my mother suffered a major heart attack at home. She was transported to the hospital where she had four more episodes over a 24-hour period. They put her in a drug-induced coma for 18 days. She spent another 30 days in intensive care, and she came out a different person. She suffered some oxygen deprivation, and two thirds of her heart stopped working, and only one third worked. It changed all of our lives. My mother was the beacon and the North Star of our family, and everything revolved around her.

She did get better after time, but she suffered from small cognitive deficits. Mom had a chance to live another 17 and a half years and was able to see all three of her sons get married, and saw her nine grandchildren. She died in September 2002. Mom was the impetus for us to create this company.

We're a solutions provider for our community, and I enjoy what we do. It's incredibly rewarding to help people navigate through the myriad of options that people are faced with when they have a loved one who is diagnosed with an illness or has an accident. I'm only as good as my people — and we have approximately 200 caregivers, with about 140 working every single day, making a difference in people's lives.

I've embraced this community and I'm part of it. I recently finished serving on the Banner Health Board, after almost 10 years. It's the largest employer in our state. In March 2017, Governor Doug Ducey appointed me to the Governor's Advisory Council on aging. I'm the first home care or home health hospice owner or general manager in its 38 years who has ever served on the council on aging. I take that responsibility seriously.

I don't measure success by the money I have in my bank account because I can tell you I wouldn't be successful there. I measure success by how rewarding the work is that we're doing and how much it fills my cup as it relates to purpose. I wake up every morning feeling engaged and ready to start the day. I go to sleep knowing that I'm caring for probably somewhere between 110 to 120 clients who need care at night, and I've got caregivers making them able to age successfully and safely in place. My passion bucket is full, and it's overflowing, as I am passionate about what I do.

The habit that contributed most to my success is the fact that I'm genuinely interested in our team and the work that we are doing every day. I don't sit up in an ivory tower. When my day gets started, I'm talking to the team members. Sam

Walton was famous for doing that, and while I'm not running a merchandise mart or grocery store and we don't have a big staff, I'm interested in my staff and their lives. They're people, and they have families, and we spend more time with them than we do with our families.

Important habits include leading by example, being willing to get my hands dirty, standing for excellence and making sure that people realize that I'm an expert in my field. I've got to work on them to get them to trust me. I want them to be able to follow me, and if that means following me into a fire, I want them to know that they are following a leader.

Lastly, an important habit is to tap into the emotions of my team. Using those emotions to drive my team is essential. I need to take care of my people, and I need to make sure that I know what's going on, and sometimes no words are being said, but I can see the body language. And I need to be able to assess that with an intuition that might come with years of experience.

One of the things that we're challenged with is workforce and finding people. For a tender spirit, a caring person, it's not about wiping butts; it's about companionship. We know that 92 percent of the surveyed people aged 65 years and older want to age in peace. Some of them need a little bit of assistance, maybe with getting dressed or help with a meal.

In the U.S., nearly one third of our population 65 and older live at home alone. They either have chosen to live at home alone, or they're widows or widowers. In couples, when caring for one another at 65 and older, 63 percent of the time, the caregiver predeceases the care recipient. If you know somebody who's a family caregiver, don't wait for them to ask you for help and please don't ask them for help — just do.

DAN MORRIS

President/CEO, Advantage Controls

www.advantagecontrols.com

We're a family-owned, family-operated enterprise that provides water treatment supplies. We operate under the golden rule of treating others as we'd like to be treated, and that's our driving principle.

My habits have played a considerable part in the success of Advantage Controls. We started with four people, so it was critical to make the right moves to kick off a successful company. Probably the most prevalent habit is just coming to work every day and feeling guilty if I didn't. Some of that is maybe just the Puritan work ethic, but showing up every day is important, and that's something a lot of people don't get. Many people have the mistaken idea that someone goes into business so he can have all those freedoms and do what he wants. Maybe, ultimately, people get to that point, but it's easier to have a job than it is to have a business because with a job, people go home at night and can then shut it off.

I'm the youngest of nine children. I'm younger than the next child by seven years; my mother was 42 when she had me. My parents didn't go to college, but they were both extremely intelligent people. They did a lot of reading, and they encouraged all of us to go to school. By the time I was in high school, they'd had children for some 40 years, so they weren't on me about it, but it was just instilled in our family that you did better, you worked hard, you wanted to go to college or you wanted to join the military.

My dad was a salesman, and he raised nine children on commission sales. Growing up, the last thing I wanted to be was a salesman. It took me a while to admit it to myself, but I was good at selling. Whatever it was I was selling, I always was good at it, even though I wouldn't admit it to myself. I finally realized that I'm a salesman, and that's what I do, so I embrace that.

We're the winners of the Oklahoma Manufacturing Leadership Award, the Business and Industries Award for social media for the web, the Governor's Small Business Award of Excellence, and the U.S. Department of Commerce's Export Achievement Award. One of the things that we're big on doing here is being involved in the community. That's extremely important, and for many reasons, not just because it's the right thing to do, but it's the right thing for our business as well.

We do blow our own horn about the things that we do to encourage our people, and part of that is recognition, so that goes along with blowing our own horn. I even tell our customer-service people that if they do something out of the ordinary for a customer, don't make it a routine, make sure the customer understands that they did something out of the ordinary. That's what people have to be told sometimes; that "Hey, what you're getting is special." That's why we promote that, plus I will admit that I have an ego, and I like to see success stories or stories about our company, so we also look for opportunities to put ourselves out there.

We've always promoted involvement in official organizations. We've always paid the club dues for Exchange Club or Rotary if a team member wants to join. We've encouraged that for a long time, and that involves them being part of charity projects. We also do a monthly luncheon where we recognize anniversaries, and we select the team's most valuable player, which is the equivalent of the employee of the month, but we don't call them employees; we call them team members. One of the components of that is some involvement within the community or the local church that involves looking beyond themselves.

There's a little food pantry about a half a mile from here, and we've been supporting them for nearly a year. People will bring in donations of food, and we get excellent feedback and some lovely stories of how people have been personally helped, and then we bring that information back to our people to help them feel better.

We do a monthly birthday party at one of the local nursing homes. We have people that are storm chasers. We're on the boards of both the United Way and Rotary. We have a guy running for state legislature, as well as volunteer firefighters and Sunday School teachers.

We do a yearly litter patrol when we get everybody out here on a Saturday, and we feed them hot dogs, and we then pick up litter. We do events. For example, during the eclipse here in our little town, we rented a Second World War submarine and had food trucks come out, and brought all our people out there on buses to watch the eclipse from the park and paid them to be there. Those are some of the things we are involved in. Our encouragement and that of our team members seeing the things that we do is changing lives. We try hard to involve everybody.

We're part of the local Chamber of Commerce, and they had an event last week called Public Service Appreciation Week.

The chamber and whoever sponsored it (and we were one of the sponsors) brought breakfast to public servants throughout the week. I decided that it would be cool to go to the fire department because I know some of the guys. I wondered who should I bring with me from the office. We have this one young man who started about two and a half years ago. He's in his mid-twenties, and since starting here, he's joined the volunteer fire department in his little town. Right after he joined, there was a tragic fire where a young mother and a child were killed, and he went through a lot of struggles and trauma afterwards about it but made it through. I didn't know him on a very personal level, but he was the guy I picked to go to the breakfast with me.

As I was driving down there, he started talking as if he'd written it down and rehearsed it like he was in a play, but I knew it was from the heart. He said when he started working for us, he never would've conceived of doing work and not getting paid for it. He said working at Advantage Controls has changed his life. I get choked up just telling this story about him. I don't know how many people, how many lives he's going to touch, and that's going to be a direct result of the way that Advantage Controls has touched his life. That's very powerful.

LYNN ARRINGTON and DAVID WATKINS

Co-Founders, Arrington Watkins

www.awarch.com

I think neither of us felt like we could be successful in this venture by ourselves, but together we have different skills, and we're compatible, and we thought we could make a go of it.

We started Arrington Watkins in 1994 after the architectural firm we'd worked for disbanded. Within a year, we had ten people and a $200 million project that had been awarded us by the state. That set us on the right path. The company has now been sold to seven people who worked with us for a very long time. We'd been in business since 1994, so we hired four of them then. We groomed them over the years to be leaders and owners. When that took place, which was last September, it was fairly invisible. We stepped aside; they took over what they'd been doing for quite a while. Many people don't even know, which we think is probably a good thing.

We knew selling the company was the right thing to do. Emotionally, it's been difficult to give up our baby and what we love doing and do something different. It was, however, the right time for everybody involved. We formed another little company called Sage Concepts where we provide services to some clients. We don't do traditional architecture because we would give those projects to Arrington Watkins, but we do client representation, master planning and architectural programming. So we kept busy.

We moved from their offices into a room together so that we could work together and be our own little company. But it's in the same office building as Arrington Watkins. We come to work every day, but we don't stay until 7 p.m. anymore. We keep in touch with what's going on in the office, and they're doing very well. They announced yesterday that they got four new jobs without going through competitions. They were awarded directly to them because of our reputation and that's unusual.

We're enjoying it. We're still doing what we like to do and that's to develop clients and projects. Now we do it on behalf of Arrington Watkins so they can be successful. We've got our hands still in the procession. We're learning some new tricks for old dogs, and life's good. We don't have the pace that we had. If we want to play golf or we want to take an afternoon off, we can do that now which is quite a bit different. One of the things that we always did was we worked as hard or harder to get data to work for us. So we were putting in the hours. We're glad the transition took place. We're proud of the fact that we pulled that off. We've not seen many successful architectural sales and transitions done internally. A lot of them get done by big companies buying up small companies. Even then, though, their success is going to be tenuous. So we're proud of having done that as it looks like it's been successful.

"David and I worked together for 17 or 18 years at another firm," Lynn said. "We went to the same college together. We didn't know each other, but we thought a lot alike even though we were completely different in our personalities. I'm the out-of-the-box guy, and I need to be reined in and kept in line. David's a good organizer and a good businessman and the perfect partner."

"I couldn't do alone what Lynn and I have done together," David said. "I was able to lend my best self to the company because Lynn was doing the part that I probably would have had trouble with. We had to be willing to take risks, but every risk we took was a calculated risk. I felt like we would never fail because we had thought it through and it made sense. We took a risk when we started the company and walked away from our jobs. It's wrong to take stupid risks but to do what we've done we had to take a risk. We had to make sure, however, that it was a calculated risk."

"Whatever the partnership is," Lynn added, "it has to have good business sense. Too many architects are architects for the challenge of architecture and design and lose track of the business. If we didn't pay attention to the business, then it'd catch up with us. I've been blessed to have David with that talent and that focus as it's essential to a successful firm."

When we started our firm, we decided not to have debt. That's what killed the other company. It's not that there's not a place for debt; however, in architecture and the building industry, the economy goes up and down sharply. We didn't survive that first up and down in the late 1980s at our other company. We had never experienced that before, so the senior management of that company didn't know how to handle that and they had much debt, and it went under. We went through one significant downturn in 2008, and we survived it because we had no debt and we had a cash reserve, and we were able to keep a team together.

We committed to running the business like a business, so everything that we did, we would ask if it was good for the company or just good for some individual. We also set an example for everybody. We didn't act like prima donna leaders that came in late and left early. We put in as many hours as anybody and led by doing, not by words. We wanted to be role models for all the people who worked for us — a definite habit that we had.

Another critical habit was that we recognized, nurtured, and challenged talent. We had these people take over the company because we recognized that they were good. We nurtured whatever their talent was, and we challenged them. We put people in positions that other firms wouldn't because we judged whether they had the talent and then we said we would give them more.

We always looked at everything thinking that there's got to be a better way. We can do what we do, but there's got to be some way to do it a little different or a little better. That drove us to try to find better solutions. We never had a closed-door policy. Our offices were always open, and people could come and go anytime they wanted to meet with us and talk with us.

We developed early on a vision for Arrington Watkins with 12 items on it. One of the things we live by and maybe the most important tenet out of those 12 is that we're a service business and we realize we're a service business. We wanted to provide the service so that everybody that we worked with, whether it was owners, users, consultants, or lenders, would react, "Wow. Those guys are good." So we would say that we wanted to provide wow service. We did, and that was largely what made us successful.

BRUCE TYREE

Owner, Great Lakes Fireworks

great-lakes-fireworks-2.myshopify.com

We get more from people through love than we do with hate.

I don't know if there's anything as a young person that helped me career-wise other than that I was adventurous and liked to take on challenges. When we're young, and we do those types of things, we find out that we can make those successes, and we can succeed and overcome some of the challenges we find ourselves in. It helps us further down the road to have more confidence in what we're doing.

I grew up by a lake, so I water-skied all the time. I can remember always wanting to be better and trying all types of different things to be more successful. I had the drive to be better. I'm good at keeping myself motivated.

Many of my employees and people that I've worked with tell me that I'm the most easy-going boss they've ever had. People don't want to let me down because of the respect I show to them, so they give that same respect back to me. They don't want to let me down, rather than worrying they're going to get their butt chewed. That's a powerful difference and that's probably what makes a good leader.

It's important to understand that respect is earned. It's not something I can demand — and it's mutual. It can be difficult for leaders to know how to show respect to those who are in a subordinate position to them without losing that sense of leadership — and that's a beautiful, delicate balance to achieve. People will look up to me and respect me because I show them respect.

Working in pyrotechnics might seem like an inherently fun job. That's the way it was at first, just like anything. Every job is, though, still a job, and a lot of the people who work for me enjoy it because a lot of them work part-time. They work on weekends for example when we do fireworks displays. Most of my people have their jobs, and they're just weekend warriors for me. A lot of them take their vacation time during the summer so that they can work fireworks displays because they enjoy it.

When we have that successful display, it's a great feeling, and we feel that sense of accomplishment. During May and June, however, as we head into the summer, we will have more than 100 displays that we have to coordinate and promises that we've made to our customers. The stress can be quite overwhelming at times.

I probably developed my leadership style through experience. Growing up, I had many jobs myself. I worked for many people, and I knew how I felt, and how I liked to be treated. I try to reflect that back onto the people who work for me by leading with empathy and compassion.

It's powerful, and it shows in how my employees feel about me. They don't want to let me down. They don't want to disappoint me. I don't want them to feel like some of my old bosses made me think. There's a powerful lesson here for young entrepreneurs; for young people just getting started. Those terrible jobs, and those awful bosses, if nothing else, show us who we don't want to be.

My attitude and outlook and the way I look at things has a significant role in my success. Having a solid work ethic and not being afraid to take those leaps or set those high goals might cause some to ask why we're doing all that; why we're giving ourselves all that extra work or putting all that additional stress or pressure on ourselves. For me, however, I feel that if there isn't a little stress in my life, I'm not pushing myself hard enough.

JOHN HERNANDEZ and RON MERITT
Co-Owners, On Advertising
on-advertising.com

Ultimately partnerships come down to respect and understanding that the business always comes first.

"As my habits go, I don't like to beat around the bush," John said. "I'm straight to the point when it comes to business, and I approach business in an unemotional way. Ron and I are absolute opposites, so we play off each other well. My habits are the opposite of his habits, and they work well together. We've seen many partnerships dissolve because one was adamant they wanted it one way, and one was adamant they wanted it the other way. They put their personal beliefs above the business. We measure our likes and dislikes and what we think a good direction is. The business always comes first, and there always has to be a compromise. One way or the other, if we're in a disagreement, we'll agree for the sake of the business."

"I would classify myself," Ron said, "as the politically correct individual where I walk and talk what clients expect to get from an agency such as ours. I tend to be that mediator, the person who tries to control expectations and set specific parameters and goals based on realistic timelines. I do that not only with our clients externally but also internally with our employees and even myself. My habits are that of being very scheduled, fairly rigid, and always having a set goal that must be accomplished that particular day. My personal and my professional habits go hand in hand."

"It's not a matter of keeping either one of us in check; it's a matter of respecting our boundaries and respecting each other's time and of understanding what each person is doing within the agency," Ron explained. "John handles our budgeting and financing and growth development, and I handle our day-to-day operations within the agency. So he understands what he's doing, and I respect that, and vice versa. That's how we have been able to become not only great partners but good friends over the past years. We've been in business now 24 years as a company and John's been with the company since 2002. That's unheard of in partnership situations like this. We have to be able to respect each other's boundaries to be successful."

"If there's an issue," John said, "the buck stops in my chair. I have to have my finger on the pulse of everything going on in the agency including the oversight of the employees at all times because there are so many moving parts in an advertising and marketing firm such as ours. If it weren't for the fact that I'm very rigid with my time and am task oriented, we'd probably be in a different position now. We have to have discipline, we have to have measured goals on a daily basis, and we have to have a strong leadership approach to employees because of the number of companies and individuals that we are working with at any one time."

"I was a television producer for a long time," John added, "and I usually had a staff of anywhere between three and 20 people depending on where I was working. There's a way of doing things, as far as getting people on board with what we're trying to accomplish, as television is a tough business where there's a lot of screaming and yelling. There are a ton of egos, and my approach was very different as I went through the business of trying to get everyone on one team instead of an 'us against them' mentality. I take that same mentality to business that we're all a team working for the same thing."

"From a CEO standpoint, we're not a typical business," John explained. "I'm certainly not a typical CEO. We run our business the way it works for us in the best way possible. Our employees seem to grasp our vision and our enthusiasm and just the way that we work together as partners."

"Over the years, it's been a challenge for me," Ron said, "but I'm slowly getting to the point where I can know that once I delegate work to other employees, they're going to get it done just as productively as if I had done it myself. It's one of those things where it took more time for me to learn that particular lesson than it probably should have."

As owners, we always have to be working in our business to make sure that the claims are getting the proper care, and the goals are met as an agency. As owners, we should be working on the business all the time.

We have fun working on and in our business. Before either of us speaks, he asks himself what their feelings are; what are their thoughts; what direction are they trying to take; how he can help them; how he can make changes; and whether there are personality clashes. We try to measure all that before we jump into a conversation. We've had many conversations about how we want to run the business. We said that everything that television did to us as employees, we were not going to do to our employees. We just did a complete about-face on how we're going to treat people and how we will respect them.

"My door is always open unless I'm on a phone call," John said. "That's had a big effect on the employees. Especially when I'm interviewing staff, and I say, 'Hey, your desk is going to be two desks away from mine, and all you have to do is stand up and talk to me or come over to my desk.' As an owner, when you have that kind of transparency, it works."

STEVE KANTOR

Founder, Medical Solutions Supplier

www.medsolsupplier.com

I have a habit of trying to see the best in somebody, and it has served me well.

I'd known Joe Carberry socially, and as our friendship grew, I saw something in him that inspired me to ask if he wanted to build my sales force. Though he knew little about the industry or the product, he spent the next six months learning everything that I knew about the industry and the product, and he proceeded to build a sales team. Now, 14 years later, we're a company of some 70 people with 25 sales representatives throughout the country. We are now the largest distributor of the Lympha Press compression-therapy device in the United States. A key to my success has been attracting quality people like Joe who have become excellent partners and who have inspired our workforce to believe in one of the most important components of Medical Solutions Supplier — our corporate culture.

One of my favorite books is Stephen Covey's *The Speed of Trust*. Developing that trust takes time, but it's worth it. Joe and I have a great relationship; it's almost like we know what the other is thinking. We're always headed in the same direction, though we may have different ideas regarding how to get there. Because of the level of trust we share, there's great openness; conversations are candid, and I have the freedom to allow him to run my company.

I'm a people person. As a child, I was easy going and got along with almost everyone. In the part of Brooklyn where I grew up, families were in a similar income bracket, though culturally diverse. This background served me well; it caused me at a young age to understand that some people are different and think differently. I learned to read people and communicate with those who may not always have the same ideas or values as my own.

My approach is simple. Everyone starts as a rock star. I believe in them; I believe everybody is great and that they're going to do a great job. They must prove me wrong to fall off that initial pedestal.

My leadership style revolves around an inquisitive openness which I express to staff as "I don't know. What do you think?" It empowers my managers to exercise their brilliance. I'm encouraging them to think for themselves. Everybody in the company knows that their opinions are valued, and that's not lip service. Every conversation is an opportunity for both sides to learn.

The underpinning of our culture is appreciation. As a leader, I believe in taking responsibility and liberally giving credit where it's due. By creating a safe place where creative problem-solving can flourish, and new ideas can thrive, our people aren't afraid to make mistakes. They know they won't be chastised because mistakes are an opportunity for us to look at a process rather than the person. Encouragement is the baseline when it comes to both successes and perceived failures.

Our culture is wrapped around good teamwork through which a mix of talents and skills combine to move us forward. We have created an award-winning atmosphere (in 2018, Medical Solutions Supplier was ranked the #19 Small Business in America by *Fortune* magazine) where individual styles can thrive, but everyone is aiming for the same target.

As a kid, I was 100 percent a sports fanatic. I couldn't stay inside the house. I needed to be outside; I needed to play ball. That also helped develop my approach in business because I couldn't play ball by myself! There was always teamwork involved and I played with boys that were at different levels of ability. Working together as a group meant that each person was able to contribute something to the game.

In work, everybody comes to the table prepared to bring something. They may not even be clear on what that is until you encourage them to be curious, and let them blossom. Beyond the corporate world, this approach to life enables other valued relationships to bloom, whether in our social life or our family life.

When I believe in people and prove by my actions that I do, it encourages them to bring out the best in themselves. I don't believe in an iron fist. I've always felt that, by example, I could inspire people to do the right thing, which is what my grandma always taught me. With that as my barometer, I know I'm going to succeed.

TOM KLEINHENZ

Founder, Co-Owner and Executive Director, Rehab Assist, Inc.

www.rehabassist.com

A business is like a marriage. It's just as important for us to be successful in our partnerships and our communication as it is in our young lives and young marriages.

It's been quite a journey for my business partner and me. Buddy Brennan and I met more than 30 years ago when we were both in the field of brain-injury rehabilitation. We are both clinicians. He has a master's degree in speech and language pathology, and I'm a nurse by training. We had different and varying roles when we were in the business and the field of brain-injury rehabilitation. When we started Rehab Assist, we honestly thought we were initially going to be consulting with the insurance industry, so we had a model for our company in mind, and it didn't quite go in that direction.

Perhaps one of the habits Buddy and I share is our stubbornness, our perseverance and our ability and willingness to rediscover who we are and what we could bring to our industry at large — the disabled population. We initially started the company as two friends and two colleagues, who in the beginning didn't know whether or not the company would be able to support one, let alone two of us. Today we are a company of 15 in the Chicago metro area. I guess that's maybe a description of success to some extent.

Certainly, hard work is also a habit we share. I'm a child of the Midwest, born to hard-working middle-class parents in southern Wisconsin. I'm the second of six children, with nine years' difference between the six of us. Buddy is one of eight children and the son of a Chicago policeman. So we come from similar backgrounds.

A sense of hard work and follow-through and loyalty are elements in our success. We both have the tenacity to persevere and go through tough times. Self-competing is another aspect as often I'm not satisfied with the result that I put forth. That spurs me on to do better; better in a future endeavor with a similar project; wanting to strive to succeed; wanting to be the best at what I'm doing. Those are attributes, and I think that those are characteristics that describe me and are attributable to Buddy as well.

When I was growing up, the sense of working hard, being responsible, having chores, and having duties was a necessity. There wasn't any slacking off. Buddy and I both share the habit of working hard but taking a tentative approach to things. Rather than casting all of our fate to the winds and jumping into things, we've made small steps, or we've taken measured approaches. As a result, we've been in business 25 years. We have unparalleled longevity and dedication with our team and the people that have been with us.

Of course, it wasn't always that way. Because of our initial tentative approach when we started Rehab Assist, both Buddy and I thought that we were going to be consulting and offering a specialty service to insurance companies. That was the birth of Rehab Assist. So in those early days, as we were pounding on doors, we were trying to sell our concept to big insurance companies and insurance carriers that have policies and provide cover for people with a traumatic brain injury.

We made those calls and made those presentations, but nobody was buying. That caused us to rethink our whole approach and what it was that we could do for people; who we were and what Rehab Assist was. Some might argue and say it was the taking of measured steps that allowed us to become successful.

In the early years, it was difficult. Buddy is seven years younger than me. When we started our company, he was in his early thirties and was married with two small children. His responsibilities and what he needed to do for his family were one set of circumstances that propelled him, and what I needed to do with my circumstances and my family provided the impetus for me.

Buddy and I have similar temperaments regarding our approach to dealing with people. We're two different men with two different lives and two different approaches to things, but I think we are very similar. In almost 25 years of this business arrangement, I could count on one hand the times that Buddy and I have had a serious issue with one another or something that we had to sit down and iron out. So it's been a great partnership and that's so important in the success of a company.

In spite of how different we are from each other, I believe people can find a common bond. There's a need for people to be loved and to love, and to feel a sense of belonging. Despite what you have regarding assets or net worth and value, illness can cut through all of that. Whether it's physical illness or mental illness or spiritual illness, it cuts straight through, and it creates equality in people no matter what their differences are and where they come from.

PETER PREOVOLOS

Founder, Pen Checks Trust, Inc.

www.penchecks.com

No.1 in my organization are my employees. Moreover, they know that's how I feel.

My habits are significant to the outcome of anything I try to do. It affects not only me as an individual, but it affects everything I touch and everybody I deal with. Work ethic is an important habit; if I'm going to succeed, I can't watch the clock. Time means nothing other than to produce results. Do the job. Get it done.

I've had to learn to be a steward, taking care of those who work for me. Where are my priorities relative to my customers and my employees? We hear that the customer comes first, but not in my book. My employee comes first because if my employee is happy, they like coming to work. Guess what then happens to my customer. They're happy.

I make a point to talk to every one of my employees at least two or three times a week, and that means getting up and visiting them wherever they are, wherever they work and taking an interest in them. That includes their families, children, dreams and disappointments. If an employee has a problem, whether it's at home or in the office, I want to help out. I want to be part of that to see if I can help him solve his problem.

I also believe in coaching my employees. I want my employees to be better than when they came to me. I want my employees to be able to feel they can grow within the company, and if they can't improve within the company because we're too small, or not big enough yet, that if they go to somebody else, they'll be better prepared to be successful at the new job.

I don't believe in annual performance reviews. They don't mean anything. We do quarterly coaching. We look at what an employee has achieved during the quarter. It's not about criticism; it's about how we can help the employee improve. We look to make course corrects, and that can only be done if we sit down and coach each employee on a quarterly basis. It's the only time it becomes meaningful. If I wait until the end of the year, it's too late. It doesn't mean anything.

I want my employees to be better than when they came to me; to be better prepared to advance within my company, and if they can't, they will be better prepared to be successful wherever they go. If somebody leaves me, I want the inheriting organization to know they're getting a quality employee.

When I entered the workforce, I was an employee of Wells Fargo Bank. My supervisor was extraordinary. He was loving; he was caring; he gave me the room to grow and succeed. He was never critical. That's what a leader does; that's how a steward operates. He was comfortable with himself and with his world. He didn't have to prove anything, but he cared about his employees.

My father didn't believe in allowances. It was expected of me to keep my bedroom clean; to pick up my clothes, and put them in the hamper; to be polite and respectful; and pick up my dishes from the dinner table. I was already compensated for those basic obligations with food, clothing, housing and education. If I felt I needed funds, or needed something to buy other than the basics, I would have to ask my parents and have to justify why I needed it. If I didn't want to have to explain, then I had to figure out how to make some money legitimately, such as mowing the neighbor's lawn.

There are things we can do at an early age to inspire people to become successful and to be entrepreneurs. Entrepreneurship can't be taught at a four-year college. They might teach some business skills. We need to start, however, when we're young to learn responsibility and to learn to be a possibility thinker; to learn to achieve what we want to achieve. I'm not going to get a trophy at the end of the season for not winning. If I want to win, I have to work at it.

Sadly, I see young people come to work for me, and they expect to be the president of the company. It doesn't work that way. It's critical that we put our time in and learn discipline. My dad used to say to me, "When you go to work for somebody, if they want you to be at work at 8, be there at 7.30. If quitting time is at 5, you leave at 5.30. You give somebody 100 percent because if you give anything less, you're cheating them. You're stealing from them." Those are the lessons that I was taught.

I learned early how to be an excellent employee, so I recognize how to treat my own employees. I tell them that one of my biggest concerns is to make sure they can put food on the table, buy clothing, and care for themselves and their families. One of my main objectives in running all of my companies is to take care of my employees.

PETER COLLINS

Founder and CEO, A2B Tracking

www.a2btracking.com

It's extremely important to surround myself with good people.

I'm an early bird, and I'm up by about 5 or 5.30, and on the flip side, I'm fading by about 9 at night. As an early-to-bed and early-to-rise guy, my children laugh at me because I'm ready to go to bed so early.

When it's quiet before anyone else is up, it's a contemplative time of day for me. I intentionally don't look at my phone or email or any news at that time of day. I know that there's always plenty of time for that later in the morning to catch up on those things. I do my best to be as present as possible, particularly as my children are getting up. Together, my family and I prepare for the day.

I try not to make it fast-paced because the rest of the day becomes that way. I want to make sure that I see my children off to school, or see them for at least part of the morning before they head off for the day. Maybe I'll get in a workout before I head off, as that's also my time to exercise. Even if I don't get a workout, it's push-ups or sit-ups or something to get the endorphins going. Once the rituals are over, I head into the electronic stuff that dominates my day.

I've always believed that our habits define who we are, and how we operate. We rely on our good practices to keep us habitually good. The flip side of that is to try and minimize the negative or destructive habits. We're all human, and we all have negative habits. They can, however, get out of control. Maintaining positive habits is, therefore, crucial.

Leadership habits didn't come naturally to me at all. Early in my career, I had a mentality of get to work, work hard, don't bother me. It took me quite a while to come out of that and recognize that it's a team sport. It isn't about me; it's much more about broadening the inputs from all around. I had to understand that if I was going to be effective in what I did every day, I had to learn the things that didn't come naturally to me. I've been pleased with the results; however, it's hard sometimes to sort of break out of that standard way of thinking and operating. My leadership style has had to evolve.

Early in my career, I thought that I could find the answers outside, in others. I didn't quite have it in myself to make tough decisions or smart decisions. These days, I read books about tapping the inner wisdom and making intelligent choices. I've been developing a sense in my gut that it's the right decision. I've learned that when I take time to quiet things down and think about the situation, wise answers come.

There are always many factors that contribute to positive things happening. One of the things that I've learned — and it's taken me some time to learn this — is that as a leader, I have to be intentional and deliberate about recognizing my staff for all the great things that they do and take that time to appreciate them.

Early on, I recognized that the way I operated was that I'd always been my source of motivation; I never necessarily needed anyone to pat me on the back or express appreciation; I just did what I did. Now, however, I've come to realize that most people don't operate that way. Many people feed off that need for appreciation for team engagement and that connectedness. They want to know that they're doing something that makes a difference.

So it's critical for me to remember to go out of my way to communicate that. I'm sure I still don't do it as much as I should. It's the small things. It's buying the team lunch so we can all sit around and enjoy a meal together. Alternatively, from to time, I give some public recognition of a particular individual or team achievements. That affirmation makes the most significant difference.

RON KLEIMAN

CEO, BenefitVision

www.benefitvision.com

I work for my employees; they don't work for me.

People somehow think BenefitVision is in the eyeglass business. We're not. We're in the business of helping people have a better vision; a better understanding of their employee benefits.

At 74, I can tell you that I've mellowed over the years. I tend to let things slide. I have some essential beliefs which guide me though. My job is to support my members of staff; to make my employees successful by doing whatever I need to do to help them succeed in their careers. I can't do their jobs. I have more than 30 people in my I.T. department alone, and I can't do what any one of them does. I don't know how to do that stuff. I've got several hundred people working in our call centers doing enrollment, and I don't do their jobs.

The funny thing is that for all of the money we make from enrolling life insurance and other insurances — although I am a licensed agent in every state and in D.C. and Puerto Rico — I have never sold an insurance policy in my life. I wouldn't know how.

I need all these people to be successful. I need to do whatever it takes to coach them; to set up the infrastructure; to set up the systems to make them successful. If I focus on what they're doing for me, and not what I'm doing for them, we're not going to get anywhere.

Our firm is a communication firm that helps people have a better understanding of their employee benefits. We invented the enrollment process we use today and the way it is paid for. We begin with a person who explains the company's benefits to their employees through a guided enrollment process in which the employee follows along in a workbook that is designed to be interactive.

Alternatively, they can do so online, whether following along on computer screens or a co-browsing session in which we are leading them through this explanation of their benefits. There's a big problem because people turn out to be expensive. What employer is going to pay someone to spend half an hour per employee explaining their benefits? Or giving them an orientation on their benefits?

So, almost 35 years ago, I participated in making this whole process affordable through a creative funding process. We don't charge the employers or the employees. We don't send bills to anybody. It's a fantastic process. We work with an employer to find new benefits that they are not currently offering their employees — typically, permanent life insurance, critical illness insurance, accident insurance, and/or legal insurance.

We look at all the kinds of things that employees would also like to have, that their employers are not offering, and add them to the menu of what they can enroll in, along with their other benefits that fill gaps and meet their family's needs. Then we get the income from those plans in the form of a commission from the carriers, and that pays for our entire enrollment service. We don't charge the client; nor do we charge the employees.

It's a fantastic process. The employees win, and I love it. It's win, win, win. The employees get a much better benefit communication, and they get help in making informed decisions and new benefits that they like to have. The employer cuts their costs in numerous ways.

Moreover, we feel good knowing that what we do significantly reduces overhead and turnover. Replacing employees who leave is expensive, and we have proof that what we do will significantly cut the employer's turnover. We also give our clients a total benefit administration system, saving them the set up and monthly fees typically paid to the providers who sell these systems.

We help ourselves certainly, but we also support the brokers to develop more business. They are making more money off the other insurance plans that they already have in place because we get higher enrollment results than typical enrollment methods.

The part that makes me feel good is that we have more than 300 employees. One time, I was getting a cold, and my mother said to me, "Ron, you can't get sick. You have to take care of yourself. You have so many people counting on you for their livelihood, and relying on your company to be there for them."

All of these employees — who are like family to me — are feeding their own families and supporting the grocery stores, gas stations, and other local businesses; are spreading all that money, business and goodwill around their community. The ripple effect of having a successful workforce is an exciting responsibility and a sense of accomplishment. To me, that's important.

MARIO TOMMOLILLO
President, Classic Auto Body
www.classicautobody.org

As Italian immigrants, both my mother and father gave me a strong work ethic. I try to be true to what I used to be, what I am and what I will be.

My dad came to this country in 1966 as a jeweler with a working contract, and our family followed a year later. I had parents who demanded respect. They showed me the work ethic of coming to this country with the idea to have a better life for their children. They sacrificed because they didn't speak any English and nor did we when we came to this country. They instituted in me my work ethic and respect.

When we came by boat to land in New York, we were told that if we wanted to see the Statue of Liberty, we had to get up at 5 a.m. So we did. We didn't get to see it, however, because the fog was so thick that day that we couldn't see in front of our faces, let alone the Statue of Liberty. We came with the intention to adapt to a new world and we embraced it.

Our parents demanded that we go all the way through high school because their generation only attended to fourth or fifth grade at best and then they had to go to work. That's what it was like back in those days. When I graduated from high school, and I signed up for the draft in 1973 at 17, my mom was livid, and she said, "You're not a citizen, and they're going to kill you in Vietnam. That's when Nixon pulled the plug on the draft. I told her it was my obligation to the government."

It was a standard procedure in those days that my parents never asked for relief; they never asked for anything. They worked for it and earned it. So having said that, they built me the way that I am, and I'm thankful for it. For example, believe it or not, after all these years, if I shake hands with somebody, they'll never tear me from what I said I would do. To me, a shaking of the hand is quite important.

In 2014 I was awarded Business of the Year representing Passaic County. Mine was one of 13 counties in the state of New Jersey that were featured. When I had to say a couple of words at the podium, my closing statement was "I stand before you as an Italian immigrant with a high-school diploma, and I'm being honored today. I'm living the American Dream, and I'm not alone. I'm not patting myself on the back given that millions of people have done the same." In 2017, I was awarded the Faith in Paterson Award by the local Chamber of Commerce, recognizing that I've been in Paterson since I started working there in July 1976 and have never left.

Paterson is an extremely urban area, and the majority of the people here are from South America; I think 63 countries are represented here. Ten years ago I was appointed by the mayor to the Paterson Restoration Corporation and that dissolved. It's still in operation, but not as it used to be and seeing that it was not as active as it was, he also appointed me to sit at the board of Paterson's Urban Enterprise Zone. I also sit on the board of the Passaic County Technical School, and I'm the treasurer for the Colombians, an Italian-American organization which raises funds to donate to scholarships and hardship cases.

I'm incredibly thankful that I had family and friends who supported me when I took over Classic Auto Body. It was a nice way of growing a business that I was not 100 percent sure how to maneuver, so I did much reading and questioned many people. Before I purchased the business, I interviewed the owners of the body shop to pick their brain. They didn't know what I was doing, but I was picking people's minds to find out how I do this; when I do it; how to get it done. Next July will be my 25th year here, and the shop has been here approximately 40 years from the old owner, so it's an institution.

In the mornings, I go into the shop, and everybody gets a hello. Every week, everyone gets a compliment for something he or she has done. I try to keep my guys as happy as I possibly can as it pays to have my employees happy with me and for me. I'm here six days a week, and probably average 55 to 60 hours a week. My brother is here with me, and my daughter is working with us here, so I'm looking forward to possibly scaling it back a little bit. Maybe instead of 55 hours, I'll go to 40. I enjoy my business, though. I enjoy automotive. I love cars. I don't feel like I have to get up in the morning, I do it willingly.

When the opportunity arose to buy this shop, even though it was something that I'd never considered, I took it. I had the backing of the family and friends, but I was here alone. Whatever I did, however, I did it; I rolled up my sleeves, I kicked myself in the butt and said, "Alright, this is what we're going to do." I decided to work hard for seven years and then after that maybe we could slow down. Well, 25 years later, I'm working more hours than I ever did.

My parents asked us to go to high school. My dream for my daughters was for them to go through college and I can happily say that I met my parents' dream about going through high school and that both my daughters went to college. I look at my parents every so often and say, "Hey, guys, I'm doing okay. Your dreams? I think I've met them, and even went a step further in many cases". I called my mom and my dad when my youngest daughter graduated from college and said, "This is the first Tommolillo to graduate from college in the United States". I felt extremely proud of that accomplishment.

JOSEPH WYRICK

President and CEO, EWR, Inc.

www.ewr-it.com

It helps to turn everyone into collaborators, so everyone's part of the process. If we're working together, we have to be courteous to solve problems and have new ideas.

There are four business-related habits that have been vital to the success of my company. The first thing I do every day — whether it's been a good day or a bad day — is to give thanks to God for the day. I say, "Thank you for just letting me make it through one more day". There are many days when that helps a lot.

When the company was new, almost every phone call was from somebody who was mad about something. That, however, isn't the case today, but back then, that support was essential — everybody I talked to was aggravated. The computer wasn't working right. I supposedly had lost their data. Sitting down for a few minutes every day and being thankful for my blessings helped enormously. That one was essential, as it certainly kept everything sane. When everybody's going crazy around me, if I can keep my head, and even when people are yelling at me, there are still blessings out there.

I had a man call and say he was in the Bootheel of Missouri and it would take him about two to three hours to get to Memphis. He was so mad, he threatened to drive here, and when he got down here, he was going to beat the you-know-what out of me. Those were his words, not mine. Well, that scared the snot out of me. I told the staff, "We may have a situation and I may need your help". We locked all the doors, and everybody was on pins and needles. The man never showed up, as I'm sure he just wanted to scare the daylights out of me. I consider it a blessing that he never showed up.

The second habit is based on a maxim of Calvin Coolidge. When I worked at the Cotton Council years ago, my boss had it on his wall, and I used to read it anytime I went into his office and have never forgotten it. I've tried to make a habit out of it. The saying is "Nothing in the world can take the place of persistence. Talent will not; nothing is more common than unsuccessful men with talent. Genius will not; unrewarded genius is almost a proverb. Education will not; the world is full of educated derelicts. Persistence and determination alone are omnipotent." So I've tried to be extremely persistent and extremely determined in everything that I do. I'm not going to give up. I can overcome this. That's a critical habit to have when starting a company up, and wanting to be successful. We can't give up. We can't quit. We've got to be persistent.

I once called at a cotton warehouse in Alabama. I walked in the front door, and a woman put her arm around my shoulder like I was going to be her best friend. She was talking to me as we walked down the hall. Her office was a little bit of a maze, and she basically walked me into a big square around the office and then walked me back out the door I came in. As I walked outside, she said, "Thank you for coming", then she shut the screen door and locked it, and that was it. I never knew what hit me. I never got to sit down. I never got to talk to her. She got me in, walked me down the hallway and threw me out. I was there to try to sign her up as a customer. That day, I was not successful, but we did get her as a customer of the company. My persistence eventually paid off.

A third habit is to underpromise and overdeliver. It speaks for itself. I tell people I can do this and I make sure I never promise as much as I think I can do. I underpromise and then give them everything I said, plus a little bit more. That's caused many people to have a lot of confidence and faith in me.

I set a deadline that's a little further out in the future than I think we can make, and then I deliver early. If we're working on a project where we're paid by the hour, we always try to estimate more hours than we're going to use. Then we give our customer a pleasant surprise with a bill that's a little bit less than what he was expecting.

There are too many people who overpromise and underdeliver. I battle with my staff about this as people can have the mentality to tell them we can do everything in the world. Well, we're not going to do that. We're going to say to them we can do this and we're going to know in our heads and our hearts that we can do just a little bit more. Then we're going to try our best to do everything plus just a little bit more.

The fourth habit is to treat others the way I want to be treated; that includes my customers and my staff. With customers, it's easy to understand; I'm supposed to be nice to my customers. I can't yell at them, even when they're yelling at me. So we've come up with a couple of techniques that work that keep our folks under control and keep their cool. This also applies to members of staff; they like to be treated like adults, not like little children.

When I hire people, the first thing I tell them is that we hire adults, not children. The staff has great freedom to do what they need to do. If they need it and don't abuse it, they're free to leave the office and do things outside the company. We treat them as adults and let them express their ideas. Moreover, they have good ideas, as I don't have a monopoly on ideas; many of them come from the staff.

Keeping my promises is part of the way I'd want to be treated. If I promise someone something, she'd want me to keep my promise. If she promised me something, I'd want her to keep hers. That's treating people the way I'd want to be treated. That turns people into collaborators because the customer gives me ideas that I may not have had. Members of staff also come up with good ones. We don't care where they come from, just as long as somebody comes up with them.

Finally, I've got to have a little bit of passion thrown in there too. If I'm not excited about it, I'm going to have a tough time getting that engineer, computer programmer or accountant excited about my projects. That passion for solving the problem is critical as it's contagious. Passion can make it all easier. If I'm excited every day I come in, everybody else gets fired up about it too.

If I treat people the way I want to be treated, if I'm persistent, if I underpromise, overdeliver, and count my blessings every day and thank God for one more day, it becomes a little bit easier to be passionate about life and business.

JONATHAN G. GOSSELS

President and CEO, SystemExperts Corporation

systemexperts.com

Even if I have a good idea of what the right answer is, the most important words to start with when dealing with others are "Tell me what you think".

We have two tenets at SystemExperts that underlie our success. The first one is that we're all about "our" and "we"; not "mine" and "I". Certainly, I play an important role as the president and CEO, but it's the people around me that breed success. I have the same philosophy that I extend to personal, civic, sporting or professional collaborations. I can set high expectations. I can set priorities. I can provide resources. It's the team, though, that makes it come together and work.

Corporate cultures are complicated, and they reflect shared values. We feel we have a special culture. We do everything with integrity. We focus on quality and responsiveness for both our clients and our vendors. That's easy to say, but we live it day to day. One thing that differentiates SystemExperts from others is that we focus on what's essential in the world of security. Not all problems are equal, but based on our understanding of our clients' businesses, we try to distill issues to the root causes. That means they can focus their resources on solving the real problems, not abstract ones. It's easy to get buried in technical minutiae in our world, so we keep our customers grounded.

We've genuine respect for our customers. We employ staff who know what they're doing. Our methodologies are structured to build on the clients' strengths, and we model ourselves as an extension of their teams. It's a collegial approach, and never adversarial. We're not looking for a gotcha, to make someone look bad, or to find a vulnerability. It's the quiet "Hey, we found something. Here's what you've got to do to fix it".

As a culture, we're lifelong learners. We've got to be if we're going to stay at the front end of the world of cybersecurity. Everybody has to be continually pushing each other and pushing themselves. We take a long-term view of everything. It's not about the deal we're going to close tomorrow. It's not about an end of the quarter. We're privately-held, so we play for the long-term. We know that if we can overdeliver on each engagement, then the clients are going to come back when they need something done right.

Corporate culture isn't one person. It's organic. It's almost like an organism. It evolves; it changes, depending on the mix of people involved and what the stresses are on the outside environment.

I've always been disciplined. I've been a distance runner my whole life. At training, I take one step at a time in the right direction and eventually I'll finish the marathon. It's about determination; it's about having a strategy, executing, doing things well consistently, and knowing it's going to be a lot harder than I want it to be.

More importantly, it isn't just discipline but treating people right so that they know they can trust me in the long term. I'm grateful that growing up I had excellent role models and then in my professional life, I've had incredible mentors. Between family and relatives and friends and then professional mentors, I was able to learn and optimize and develop skills that have served me well.

Part of learning from mentors is they tell us when we're full of it, especially, early in a career. We come out of business school, and we think we know everything. The first thing we realize is that we know nothing. Having mentors that can tell us, "Be quiet. Listen, learn, and we'll help." We'll learn more from failure than from success. I've had a mindset that I've never been afraid to say, "I don't know," and I've never been afraid to learn from people who know better than me.

At our company, therefore, we have a sincerity aspect that's part of our culture. It's not just me treating people right; it's all of us treating our clients and vendors right. We are who we are; we don't pretend to be what we're not.

JENNIFER AMES
President, Ames Group, Chicago
www.ameschicago.com

Even the most qualified people are going to struggle if they don't come in clearly understanding what their role is, and what success looks like. A major part of the journey is learning how to do that.

I'm extroverted, and during the day I'm busy engaging people. You might think that in real estate we sell homes, but we also work to help make people's life transitions go more smoothly. That means we understand people's needs, figure out how we can help serve those needs, and ensure that when they're moving or making a change, it will go well.

I have to be a good listener. To be a good listener, I have to be present and engaged. To do that, it takes much energy. It's hard to multitask when I'm in that kind of service role, so I use my nights to organize my desk and my to-do list, send my thank-you emails, and do other critical organizational tasks.

Before bedtime, I will take a hot bath, or my husband and I will take a shower together — to turn everything off, get back, and focus. I can't bring my phone into the shower, so it's a way to shut things down. With everybody going 90 miles an hour during the day, it's a chance to turn my thoughts down, so I'm not going to bed with my head racing, and thinking all the thoughts from my day.

Running a successful business can take a lot of energy, which I feel makes the evenings that much more important. My husband and I have, therefore, created a lifestyle to make sure we can focus on each other and on our family. One is that I have a weekly meeting with my husband, and the purpose of that weekly meeting is to talk about everything and anything. This can be personal, professional, parents, household or our children.

These meetings are meant to be huge, broad-scope, open-mic events, and sometimes that can mean a three-hour conversation over brunch. We've learned that because we're both busy professionals, one of the keys for us is to have the discipline to meet once a week, out of the house, away from everybody.

We turn off our phones and that gives us a chance to organize ourselves. We block off time, plan a date night, and organize upcoming vacations. We make a plan for where we're going to go and when, how we're going to accomplish what we need with our children or with childcare, figure out who is driving, and who's taking who to camp. Because we do that, it means that I'm not distracted all the time because it's well mapped out for us.

These weekly meetings free me up to focus on everything else I need to do, and it's not like this nagging monkey on my back, telling me I need to take care of this or that. Because we've got this dedicated time, and something comes up, I can put that on the list for Sunday, and then I've cleared it.

I'm a night owl, and my husband is an early bird. Earlier in our marriage when we weren't scheduling this meeting, I'd be frustrated because I'd want to talk about something, but he would say, "Not a good time. I don't want to do it now. Let's wait till the morning." In the morning, however, he'd be up and gone, so we weren't in sync.

Making that time to be in sync is a personal thing. By having that communication platform, the conversation can be whatever it needs to be. It can be about business, an issue with a nanny or with a child. It ebbs and flows, but one component is that the conversation happens every week. We can discuss schedules, such as he is going to a guy's weekend, or one child has an event, or I'm going to attend a conference.

This helps make me more effective in my business, as a parent, as a wife and as a mother. One big challenge of being a successful person — and I see this in my work — is often when a marriage doesn't work, it's because they're not on the same page. That doesn't mean we have to have the same habits, but it says that we need to make sure that we both know what the plan is. That's the benefit of what my husband and I do, because, with our weekly meeting habit, we're always in front of the plan. We always get alignment with each other on the program. This allows us to be successful in our respective careers, maintain a healthy and close marriage, and manage a busy lifestyle as working parents with a family.

JAY JOYCE

President and CEO, The Idea People

www.theideapeople.com

If I'm responsible for building relationships, I should never leave home without the ability to listen, to smile and to empower others. A 'sale' never bought anything. The relationship does.

The three personal habits I'm most aware of are smiling, conversation and listening. While they may sound simple, in sales, we can do magic with those three skills. In management, they're critical. They can disarm others. They can motivate others. They always break the silence. They're the only and best way to build revenue; that's my motto.

I was born with those three habits, but I certainly have learned how to use them often enough so that they have become a part of me. Smiling and conversational skills came more easily to me than listening. I had to work on the listening skill until it became a habit. Every cliché about listening is so true. As a salesperson, I learn so much more, and as an employer too, by listening to the situation and people rather than by speaking and pouring out a bunch of features and benefits.

A customer will always tell me how to make the sale. An employee or a team member will always tell me what the situation is or the problem is to give me enough information to make the right decision. Having those three skills from the get-go, yet also consciously learning about what we have, is incredibly important in our company.

Listening happens to be one of the most challenging skills for people to cultivate. Because I like to converse, I have to be conscious and be aware of listening more than I talk. Clients and employees will tell me what they need through me listening to them, instead of me telling them what they need. It's hard to do but the payoff is immense.

When I graduated from college in 1985 and got my first sales position in radio advertising, I had no help other than a phone book, so I needed to find some help on how to sell. I found two books written by Spencer Johnson, *The One-Minute Salesperson* and *The One-Minute Manager* (with Ken Blanchard). These books are what I call '80/20' books, meaning that they're jam-packed with lessons rather than fluff. They helped me learn about getting 80 percent of my results from 20 percent of my effort, rather than the other way around. I still use this today.

Once I found my stride and selling style, I shifted my approach to becoming the ultimate resource for my clients while I helped them buy advertising. I also saw that listening to the clients was the key to help me build a strategy for them on the fly while building a real relationship. I still do this today.

There are no secrets to being an exceptional entrepreneur. Learning how to present ourselves, to listen to others, and to build real relationships is a big key to moving from being salespeople to being entrepreneurs.

JAY BRADLEY

President, Intelisys

www.intelisys.com

One of the key habits is continuing to learn about others. We can always get better if we genuinely believe that we can continue to get better. We must home in and strive to do so.

I grew up in a military family. We called ourselves air-force brats. We moved around a lot, and we learned a certain way to conduct ourselves, and specific protocol, and pomp and circumstance, as in military life, all those things are essential. I said, "Yes, sir" and "Yes, ma'am" to my parents — as both Southern folks and military folks — up until I was in my mid-thirties, which was when I felt like it was time to ask permission to be more familiar. Part of my upbringing as an air-force brat was that I had to ask many questions to get to know people, because every two or three years, we would move from one location to the next. That's part of how I became who I am.

The whole-life perspective in the way of habits that have allowed me to be in the great position that I'm in — the president of Intelisys — comes down to a level of authenticity with others. This authenticity allows me to connect with my team and with the folks that follow me, who believe in my mission. They must believe that I genuinely consider the mission, vision and their well-being just as important, if not more important, than my own, and that also involves, of course, a large part of the ability. Great leadership is about allowing people to see inside of the leader as a person. That's a huge part of it; that authenticity in relationships with people; that genuineness that everyone believes that the mission and vision are worthy. They must feel we will not only do good things for them but the community and the business.

Authenticity is what people crave; it's the thing that people are after to have meaning. Everybody needs to make a living, and the material things in life and being able to take care of the family and run a successful company are essential; however, people are looking for meaning and purpose, and if they believe they're following leadership that believes in what they're doing and believes in them, it makes all the difference.

It's important to spend time with staff talking about life in general. It's not only talking about business but talking about them. Part of every staff meeting I have includes talking about how people enjoyed their weekend, and what support they need in their lives. Do they have graduations or weddings coming up? Do they have a big anniversary or vacation that they're looking forward to?

Some people who have reported to me over the years weren't convinced early on as part of my team that those were critical things to discuss. Those hard-driving Type As that just wanted to do business all the time and focus on the task at hand didn't know what hit them. There I was, taking a left turn, wanting to talk about how their weekend went. Over time, they began to realize that caring about them and wanting to understand how they were doing as people was a habit. I want to take an interest in their lives.

Working with different people over the course of my life, the relationships I still have today are with leaders who showed a genuine interest in my well-being and my life as a person. The leaders who were all about the business, all about the money, all about their drive — they tend to be the people I have not been able to maintain a long-term relationship with.

As far as a habit goes, people know to expect that I'm not going to walk into the room and expect them to be robots. People have come to expect from me that I'm a genuine human being who understands that the people who work with me are also human beings with a whole life outside of the work that we're doing together. I'm going to ask questions, and want to know who they are as people and customers, not just team members.

JAMES BODINE

Owner, CJS Systems Heating and Cooling

cjsheatingandair.com

I have learned that it takes all different types of people in the workplace. We need those types of people to help us build different types of businesses. If everybody wanted to be the boss, there would be nobody left to run the business systems.

My No.1 habit that's played a role in the success of the company is that when I have free time, I work on projects. I'll take any downtime and go to work. I never say, "I just don't feel like working today." I don't ever do that; I get up and get after it. Moreover, that's my attitude throughout the day too. If there's downtime, I get after it. That's the habit that's played a big role in the success that we've had; that habit of continually working on projects or driving things forward keeps us moving forward.

I work on anything from studying acquisition, a new pricing guide, something that's going to increase the profitability of the company or the way the techs present to the clients. I seek to soften things up where clients feel a little more at ease about the way ideas are presented to them. All the time, I'm working on stuff like that or marketing strategies; deciding how we're going to go to market and what kind of approach we're going to use; all these little projects that we end up working on. There's a ton of little things that contribute to the growth of the company.

Ever since I was a kid, and I was able, I went out and knocked on doors, selling my services of taking care of people's lawns and gathering leaves; I even had garages that I kept clean for different people. This was before the working age of 16. As soon as I was able to work, I had jobs at different places, including restaurants, meat lockers and granaries. I did anything that I could do to work and be competitive, and I enjoyed it. I got something out of it, and it did something for me. It made something inside of me feel alive. I don't know if I can pinpoint where it came from, but I can tell you that there's something inside of me that gets excited. Different things excite different people. For me, it's never necessarily been about making money, although to run a great business, we have to make money, or the business won't survive. Another landmark in running a great company is that it's profitable, just as getting a great customer service score is part of running a great business.

I like to learn continually, to keep growing, overcome, and to take on things. If I don't have any stress in my life, I'm out there inventing it. There's something inside of me that craves that. I was taught a long time ago that if I take the pressure and make it negative, it becomes terrible stress. If I take the pressure and make it positive, it just pushes me forward. It becomes a positive force of energy. So the challenge is to take any pressure that we're feeling and convert that into how to move forward.

At first, I wondered why everybody wasn't like me. I started this business when I was 24, so I asked why wouldn't everybody want to be like this. I'd meet people who were just content with putting in their eight hours and weren't necessarily interested in climbing a ladder or achieving what I defined as success. As I've matured, I've realized that everybody's definition of success is a little bit different. One guy might be an athlete or a singer or just the best family man that he can be. That's his definition of success. Other people want some of those things too; however, they want to improve continually in their career or make the most money they can make, and that's their definition of success.

One of the things that make us stand out in our industry is the amount of time that we spend training our people. We have a philosophy around here as a management team that we spend 30 percent of our time recruiting, and 30 percent of our time training. So 60 percent of a manager's time is spent either recruiting or training. A lot of our training — even though we do a significant amount on technical items — is on soft skills since we're dealing with the public.

To hear the needs of our customers, we teach soft skills to our technicians. Generally, they go to school to learn how to fix things. They don't go to school to learn how to communicate at a high level with others. When we're dealing with people and their problems, we have to listen and talk at a high level, so we're happy to train our staff in those areas.

PART THREE

POSITIVE HABITS

Naturally, successful leaders will have more than a few positive habits. It only makes sense, as success is rarely an accident! When we released *Supreme Leadership* in 2018, many readers wanted to know details about the habits of those leaders. In particular, what were their positive habits? Do leaders tend to share the same practices, or is there a variety?

We were pleasantly surprised to learn that the following leaders not only had solid habits, but they identified them and were determined to capitalize on them continuously. What good is a habit if it's not practiced? Read on to see exactly what our featured leaders considered their most useful habits.

PETER BARNES

Owner, Clatter&Din

clatterdin.com

Maybe it's my Iowa upbringing, but I feel that there's a huge advantage over the rest of the competitive world by showing up, paying attention, and being responsible.

I was always a musician; first and foremost, a creative guy. I was also curious and interested in anything technical. I was in the band and jazz band at both junior high and high school, and I was close to one of my instructors in school, who helped to keep me out of trouble. It's easy to get into trouble in Iowa; he kept me on the straight and narrow; kept me interested in important things.

I had an interest in sound recording. My parents used to let me skip school a couple of days a year to record the moon missions, and I would tape the microphone to the TV and run my little Wollensak recorder. When I was in junior high, I had a paying job to create Christmas music on a little tape recorder and play it in the town square. So I used to get out of school about an hour a day to change the tape, and they paid me, and I thought it was all fabulous.

Then I went to college at the University of Northern Iowa on a small jazz scholarship. I was much into big-band jazz, and music of all kinds, including rock and roll. I joined a band and played a little bit of music in northwest Iowa, and quickly realized that if I wanted to make something of myself in that world, I should go to one of the coasts.

At 20, I packed everything I owned in a trailer, drove out to Seattle, and moved in with some friends. I got a part-time job and joined a band. Within two weeks, we started touring, and continued doing so for the next ten years.

We started playing cover songs five nights a week in bars and hotels in Canada and the Northwest quadrant of America. We did that for about three years, and then the original music scene came along, and we started playing our music, as we were sort of a punk, new-wave band. We played in San Francisco, Los Angeles, New York, Chicago and Minneapolis, and all over the country for about another five years.

I was continuing to grow my skills as an audio engineer and began to take it seriously, while still playing live music. I recorded bands and made records, and when I produced an album, that suddenly made me a record producer. I ended up producing about 30 or 40 records over the next five years. Because I was a trained musician, I also got to play on many records. I would play drums, engineer them, and produce them.

Then I got offered a job at a place called the Music Source. It was a high-end commercial music production company during the daytime, and they did rock-and-roll and jazz recording in the evening, so it was perfect for me. I had a day job, and then I could continue to make records in the evenings. I worked for this fellow for ten years and ended up running the joint.

Having some music and studio management experience, I joined with a friendly competitor, and we both left our jobs and opened up my current company, Clatter&Din, in 1994. It was a small boutique facility. My partner and I were both in the chair; both running the controls and working with the talent and the clients. The company grew to six or seven people, and I ended up deciding that someone had to run the business, so I got out of the chair and I became what I like to call the suit.

Back in the 1980s, when I was making a lot of records with rock-and-roll bands, I could get into a lot of trouble and be irresponsible. Clients would ask me why I was rarely drunk, showed up on time, had a good attitude, and why I cared. I said that it was because I had these three good habits: to show up, to pay attention, and to be responsible. Those habits are the core of my business life. It gives me a huge advantage over many people who have great skill sets, but lack that general responsibility gene, as I like to call it. That's something that's important to me. When I have a meeting, I tend to show up on time. I tend to be prepared. That's something that's quite important.

Additionally, I have a habit of following up. I'm a firm believer in a specific regimen of communication techniques. For example, when I want to have a business relationship with someone, it's vital for me to meet that person *in person*. If that's not possible, then certainly a phone call. It's so easy to miscommunicate and misinterpret what's said. I want to have that first initial contact in a way that I get as personal as possible: a handshake or sitting at coffee, where I can look the person in the eye. I pay attention to which communication medium is the appropriate communication medium for the task at hand.

Lastly, I try to listen to music on a regular basis as music and rhythm are good exercise for the cognitive brain. Music is a great way to balance out stress. I take music seriously and make sure that I spend some time listening to music a few times a week.

KEITH FULMER

President, Video Mount Products

www.videomount.com

I always try to accomplish something before 7 in the morning. It can be as simple as folding laundry or doing the dishes, but I always want to start the day with at least one accomplishment.

I'm always up by 5.30 and I enjoy the quiet of the early morning. Since we live in a rural area, it's nice to sit downstairs. We've got bird feeders, and the wildlife is running around, so I enjoy waking up to that. The quiet gives me a chance to ease into the hecticness of the day.

Positive habits usually lead to successful outcomes, so I try to keep the good stuff and rid myself of the rest of it. We use a neologism here at work called 'annoyance ridification'. We aim to get rid of the things that annoy us if we can. We can't always do that. It's easier said than done. Habits do, however, play a role in our success. If we don't have them, sometimes they play a role in our failure as well.

I had a great mom; she was a great woman who instilled a strong work ethic in me and my three sisters. She used to quote the maxim, "Whatever you are, be a good one." That's always resonated with me, so I've had that work ethic and accompanying habits since early on. Habits have to be honed constantly. We don't develop a habit and expect it always to fit every scenario. We have to learn something new every day. Because another one of my mom's quotes was "You don't know it all." She was a smart woman.

We were raised in a military household, and I have an accounting degree, so I can't discount that regimentation has played a significant role in whatever successes I might have. We were taught early about the P Principle (proper planning prevents poor performance). I was a scout growing up, and I'm still a scouter today. The scout motto of "Be prepared" has always been a good base for me to build on.

That being said, a dedicated work ethic can also never be overlooked or under-implemented. One of the reasons that I still enjoy being in scouting is that we are at a time when we need more mentors and fewer critics. Scouting gives us an excellent opportunity to be able to do that for what we hope will be our next generation of leadership. The book and the program that I still look back to a lot of times for preparedness and good habit forming are the *Scout Handbook* and the Scout Program.

I've had the opportunity to meet many people and take their recommendations with regard to some of the skill building that we had as scouts. A lot of it is about leadership. As leadership goes, I like to lean on those types of things because if we can teach a 10-year-old or a 17-year-old about leadership, then we're going to learn from that experience ourselves. We're helping to build a foundation by which they're going to have a strong moral compass that will help them create their future.

I've got two sons who are 27 and 24. My message for them is "Here's what your future's going to be. I think you're special but nobody else thinks you're special, so let's focus on that a little bit." Those are tough lessons. So I try to educate myself so that I can speak with them in more current terms.

For example, I listen to a lot of new music. I listen to a lot of old music too, but I listen to new music because music is one of those things that allows you to cross boundaries. Adults can talk to adolescents and younger adults if they understand the music, as well as some of the different cultural things they're going through. So I always try to keep myself educated, because I *don't know it all*.

E.J. DIETERLE

President and CEO, YES Partners

yespartners.com

Another thing which helped me a lot is the power of positive thinking.

We all are influenced by our surroundings, including the people we meet and the cultures, nationalities and families they come from. I grew up in Germany, but I've lived in various countries around the world, including 11 years in Asia, and I believe that wherever I'm located, the people I interact with and the cultures I interact with influence me.

I grew up in a small place in the countryside where interaction with people was crucial. I was involved with the local oompah band, the local soccer club, the local tennis club and other sport-related activities. It was always in the community and that had a significant influence on me. In addition, of course, I had full support from my family.

Later, I lived in big cities, such as London, New York, Seoul and Tokyo. Those are all huge cities and culture is different there. The support I got from growing up in the countryside has been vital to me.

The ability to view everything as more positive has personally helped me a lot. I was always able to see the glass as being half full rather than half empty, regardless of the facts. That's one habit that I know people can learn a lot from, as it can be difficult to attain that sort of mindset.

It's essential to have a balance, and balance could be from my family. It could involve physical exercise. It could also be the mental side. What has helped me is that I grew up in the countryside playing music. For me, playing music is something through which I always felt what other people feel when meditating. When I come home from work and feel stressed, I play music, and in 20 minutes, I'm wholly balanced again. Apart from having fun doing it, I treat it the way other people treat meditation. I feel it's powerful because regardless of what it is I focus on, it's something completely different. Focusing on something completely different is what meditation is at the end. I'm always surprised as to how many musicians I come across. It has also to do with the out-of-the-box creative thinking.

As a musician, I grew up playing in a typical oompah band; at that time, I played a baritone horn. I learned saxophone, clarinet and electric bass. I used to play in a big-band orchestra. Going from Germany to live in many other places — especially in Asia where it was a little more challenging to keep up with a band — I came full circle and now play the accordion at Oktoberfest.

ROBERT BARD

President, Latina Style Inc.
www.latinastyle.com

If we have a concern for the community, and it pulls at our heartstrings, we always find a way to do more.

Latina Style was the brainchild of my wife, Anna Maria Arias, who died in 2001. The magazine has always been an advocacy instrument for the Latina professional, so I needed somebody to run the magazine who could work with members of Congress, the White House, political leaders and with CEOs of Fortune 500 companies that we work with and Hispanic and women's organizations across the country.

In 2001, I took over the company for what I thought was going to be a short interim while we found the right person to be the publisher, and then I couldn't find the right person. I discovered that I liked that work better than running my own company, which was in public affairs and marketing, so I folded my company into Latina Style, and we created Latina Style Inc.

Latina Style Inc. is an empowerment company with five divisions. One of them publishes on Latina entrepreneurship, as we run the largest Latina entrepreneur network in the country. It's run under the umbrella of the Latina Style Business Series. We do four conferences across the country every year. So far, we've done 133 cities with more than 37,000 women going through the program.

We also have the Latina Style 50 program that is our program for Latinas in corporate America. We choose the Top 50 corporations for Latinas to work for in the United States. That program and the Latina Style Business Series program were both launched in 1998. The Latina Style 50 program also produces the Latina Style 50 awards and the Diversity Leader Conference that take place in Washington, D.C. It's the largest diversity conference for Hispanics in the U.S.

In 2004, I kept getting messages from some of our constituents to connect to others in other fields. For instance, the top Latina entrepreneurs didn't know the top Latina executives and vice versa. To focus on Latina leadership development, we created the National Latina Symposium to bring all the different audiences of Latina Style together. We wanted to recognize within that conference a group of Latinas that had never been recognized and still we're the only organization after all these years that has been vetted to recognize Latinas in the military service. So we presented distinguished military service awards for Latinas on active duty.

In addition to that, with work that we developed with the Department of Defense and the Department of Veteran Affairs, we were asked by the U.S. Navy if we would put together a program for returning active-duty personnel. We were going to have about a million veterans looking for jobs in corporate America. We created a program called the Latina Style Hero Program that runs within the National Latina Symposium and focuses on the re-assimilation and reintegration of veterans into civilian careers, specifically into corporate America.

On another side, we have our nonprofit arm of the company, Parents Step Ahead, which works with K-12 schools on empowering parents to be able to get engaged in children's education with the school system. The program focuses on empowering parents with financial literacy, health and well-being, and college preparation. It also works with parents to educate them on how to deal with bullying, how to deal with gang prevention, and even how to deal with suicide prevention for their children.

Working with a community where there's so much need, the more we do, the more we realize there's so much more that needs to be done, as long as it doesn't take us too far away from our path. We still focus on the working professional Latina, but we get pulled in so many different directions. We see that there is sometimes a desperate need for our help.

The Latina Style Business Series was started because we kept getting letters from people asking us to connect them with other people and give them advice on resources, so we decided to do a little networking session in Los Angeles for Latina entrepreneurs. We invited 75 women, but then we had 400 and 400 more that were not happy with us because we had to put them on a waiting list. Then it was a waiting list for whenever we came back because then we weren't planning anything else.

We got phone calls from all over the country. By the time we rationalized precisely how we could do this, we had returned to Los Angeles three weeks later, and we began the Latina Style Business Series. We've taken it to more than 130 cities across the United States. It's the most successful business development program for Latina entrepreneurs in the country.

At the same time, we have to be sufficiently aware and have relationships that are strong enough that we can find partners all over the country to help out. Everything that Latina Style does we're able to do because we have strong partnerships with Hispanic and women's organizations. We have cultivated those relationships through the years, and fortunately, we've been able to keep all those relationships on good terms. In essence, that's how we have done most of what we do.

Prior to 2000, there was nothing Latina, especially nothing professional. Nobody believed that there was such a thing as an audience of Latina professionals. We were able to carve our niche so deeply because there was no research whatsoever on Latina professionals. We had to develop all of that research on Latina professionals and Latina business owners. So that has been the journey that we've been on. Everything the company does it does because we have incredible partners and partnerships that have lasted what will be 25 years next April.

For instance, in the work we do in corporate America, we tend to follow closely every sponsor or partner that we have, whether in the news or on the stock market. We want to make sure that we know what's happening with their company so we're aware of changes or opportunities that exist for them and for us to work together.

Once we define what we plan to do, we must be able to stay with it. I have a postcard on a refrigerator magnet that shows a tree that's bare. There's nothing on it except a red apple. The text says, "Most of the time success means that you hung on until the end." We have to be careful how we choose our battles, but once we engage in our battles, we have to give it everything.

RICHARD MUSKUS

President, Patriot National Bancorp and Patriot Bank, N.A.

bankpatriot.com

Someone doesn't necessarily have to have his own company to be an entrepreneur.

In college, I was the guy who started doing my classroom work at about 11 o'clock at night and would finish at 2 or 3 in the morning. I was a night owl. Now I try to get enough sleep, and sometimes that means working late at night, and sometimes it means getting up early in the morning. I manage my schedule accordingly, particularly when I'm on vacation. I have to be flexible just because I never know what's around the corner. That's true for entrepreneurs because we're on call 24/7. We have that type of mentality here at the bank because we do what we have to do when we have to do it.

My habits have been critical to my success, and one of the words I use a lot around here is consistency. The consistency of my habits, meaning being predictable about where I am in the morning and where I am throughout the day, ensures everybody knows where I am and what I'm doing. Being reachable and accessible and keeping the machine moving is important for me.

Various habits I have rotate around that practice of consistency. Take communication, such as I have the method of returning emails promptly and being someone who is accessible to everyone in the company. I have an open-door policy.

We're not a big company — we're only about 125 people — but I spend as much time as I can dropping in on people. It becomes essential to be visible in areas in which a president maybe usually isn't visible, particularly when it's a bank with multiple locations.

In most cases, people know exactly where to find me, and if they don't, certainly somebody does. When I have time off, I may not be generally accessible, but there have been times when we have an aggressive loan machine that's time sensitive. There are large deals that we get involved with, and my input has been critical over the years. I was chief lending officer at the bank for a period, so being able to maintain a responsive posture on a daily basis is always essential.

I try and anticipate certain things. If I'm not going to be able to respond promptly, I make sure that I try and get enough information up-front to be able to answer. I'm typically reachable, but there are lots of situations across the bank for which I stress the ability to have someone as a backup. I emphasize the need to make sure that if I'm generally not available, I must find times when people can have access to me.

There are probably not a lot of places on the planet I can't respond from, but those are the types of things we have to be conscious of to keep our business moving. If we lose one deal, we lose two deals, and then people talk. The deals we do are our best advertising. We have to be conscious of how that could potentially affect our business.

What has happened here at Patriot Bank has been an evolution of a management team, as the people who have joined our team over the years have joined with the right mental attitude. The structure I've been professing for so long has been a lot of camaraderie, cooperation and an emphasis that we do well when the bank does well. We have a supportive group of senior executives at this bank.

We work to help one another and solve problems for one another. We all have our direct responsibilities but uniting that group of people to row in the same direction isn't as easy as it may seem. There are many problems that involve folks who may be outliers and troublemakers and people who are more concerned about themselves than the team. I'm proud to say we have an attentive, reliant, friendly group of senior executives. We're all here for the same mission, and we pick up the slack for one another. It's a dynamite set of circumstances for Patriot.

We're only as good as the people who work for us. We reward people. We inspire people. If everybody shares the same vision, we at least have a very good shot at being successful as a company.

PAUL BECKHAM

Chairman and Co-Founder, Hope Beckham, Inc.

www.hopebeckham.com

Two habits I developed were being persistent and being honest.

My dad was into dimes as he had a couple of five-cent and ten-cent stores. My brothers and I would have to work in those stores, and our dad looked to us to do the right thing. As a boy, the people that I admired, and the people that I wanted to follow, seemed to have the same idea of how to do things that I was developing at that time.

I made sure that I showed up when I was supposed to show up. I had to sweep that front sidewalk of my dad's shop, but I hated cleaning it. I had to do it every morning. I was expected to be there when needed. Christmas Eve for us was not typical, because at the stores, people would put toys and gifts on layaway. My dad would keep the stores open on Christmas Eve until the layaway items were picked up, which could be as late as midnight. The people would come in late, as they wanted to wait until the children were in bed, and they'd come to the store, and we'd have to run up and down those steps and get the layaway items, bring them down, and give them to the people.

It was interesting that my dad's view relative to bicycles and wagons and baby buggies and strollers was that they were toys and you never sold a toy in a box; you sold them entirely assembled. I grew up putting them together as he felt that if you sent a bicycle out in a box, somebody could lose a bolt or something, and they'd bring it back and want their money back. If we put it together, it was right when it went out the door. I became proficient at that sort of thing. It's not that I wanted to be there putting all that stuff together or running up and down those steps on Christmas Eve, but that's what I did.

Later, to become a lifeguard, I had to take courses in high school. We had to get to the pool early. We got to school at 7 in the morning, and then were taught life-saving techniques over a couple of days. Then we served out the rest of that day as apprentice guards. After a few days, we became lifeguards, and that's what we got up early to do.

The military was the same way. When I was in the army reserves on active duty, I got up early to learn how to do things. The whole idea was for me to learn how to do the job so that the sergeant would get off my back and I'd progress, and I'd be promoted. The same is true at work. I may have to come in early, get some stuff done, and learn it, so I get promoted, or maybe somebody else could do it.

I used to tell my children that the main thing they needed to focus on when they got out into the world was to care about what they did. If they cared about it, their focus would be on it. Because they cared, they'd be so far ahead of most people that they probably would become successful in what they did. I've always followed that myself. I cared about what I did, I wanted to do it right, and that may be the biggest thing that I tried to do.

Nothing's ever perfect all the time. I have to work my way through it or out of it if I don't care about it. Because if I care, I show up, right? I show up to where I need to be. I'm there. I'm part of it. I do all that because I care. Participation is essential, but it comes naturally if I care about what I'm doing.

I need to be honest. I need to be ethical. Some of the problems that we've seen in the business world since the recession of 2008 came about because people didn't care. They were in it for the wrong reasons, and there wasn't a sense of ethics to guide what they did. That even led to some dishonesty. Running a company, I need to be as ethically right as I can possibly be.

The problem with ethics is that there's not always one right answer. If it's an honest deal, it's probably about how I figure out what the answer is. Ethics can be shades of things. I need to take the high road and be honest with my employees.

TODD MOZER

CEO, Sensory

www.sensory.com

At Sensory, we have got to think out of the box, and I would say that's a habit for me.

Habits cross many spectrums of my life. My relationships with my friends and my family are very important. My other priorities are my health and my business. Habits play roles in all of those things. With health, I have had more intentional kinds of habits, such as what I eat and my fitness routines as opposed to family and work, but even in family and work, I have many practices.

I'm a creative out-of-the-box thinker. We're licensing technology, and we're licensing technologies that Google and Amazon and other companies give away for free, so we must be very creative. We have to be one step ahead. I'm obsessive about everything I do. I've been intentional in my obsessions. I'm proactive. I don't sit back and watch things happen.

As a small company, our most significant advantage is moving fast, thinking about work all the time and being proactive. I'm involved. I'm passionate about what I do. I test our technology religiously. Every new tech that we come out with, I play with it and learn to use it. For example, I go out walking on the streets, trying out speech recognition in different environments.

Some things I would say I had as a child, but my habits have evolved. One of the things that I try to do is to be fair to our employees and our customers and our stockholders, and I'm a believer in the win-win approach to all people that we're involved with, and I don't think I had that approach as a kid. I've always been a business person. As a kid, I had lots of businesses, but then it wasn't a long-run game where I tried to do win-wins. I just decided to buy low and sell high.

I've done much learning over the years. One of the most challenging things is managing people, and one of the things I've learned is I'm not a big believer in annual reviews. I have my people do that more as goal setting, but for my direct reports, I don't even give a yearly review. I'm a believer in constant feedback. If I were to sit down with somebody once a year, and tell them what they're doing right and what they're doing wrong, they wouldn't take well what they're doing wrong. It's a lot easier for me to be involved throughout the year and not save the bad news up, but deliver it live, so that's something that I've adopted over the years.

I go to Stanford Sierra Camp. It's a camp at Lake Tahoe, and one of the people who attends in the same week as I do is a professor at Stanford, and he was working on a book that had something to do with reviews. I don't remember the exact topic, and he started talking to me about what I do, and I said, "You know, I'm not conventional. I have this weird philosophy." I told him about not doing annual reviews, and he said that the new way of thinking about it is the way I do it, so I guess I was maybe a little bit ahead of my time, but that seems to be the way things are going.

SCOT LOISELLE

Principal, L2M Architects
l2marchitects.com

I commit time and resources and priorities to prioritize taking care of myself physically and mentally. It puts me in a better place to take care of other people as well. It comes from the expression "Pay yourself first".

One of the best ways for me to prepare for the day is by going to the gym first thing in the morning. I go at least four days a week and I kick back with less structured activities at the weekend. I find that I have more focus and energy on workout mornings. I've been doing this since college and figured out a rotation to get a good block of cardio and strength training in a two-hour workout. It's high intensity with few rests. I rely on sequencing different muscle groups so that I can push through more sets in the same amount of time.

A willingness to accept responsibility has been crucial over the years. The focus is on finding solutions as opposed to dwelling on identifying blame or fault. There's time for forensics after the project is back on track. It's critical to respect other people's ideas and to be willing to evolve in my view relative to listening and understanding often different perspectives. Acting confidently has been important as well. I use the expression 'acting' in the sense that I am not immune to self-doubt. I'm my hardest critic. Recognizing that also helps me see the value of a leader or an owner carrying a confident demeanor. It provides a context for decisions and discussions.

Practicing humility (though it's a conscious effort sometimes to challenge myself through introspection) and being a critic of my motivations and my behaviors and reactions to those around me are essential to staying grounded.

I have a concept of evolving and resilience. I'm continually seeking to be a better version of myself and hoping to help others to improve. Being in the office and being present is crucial in the sense of being available for staff and and reinforcing our culture and expectations by being there ourselves and participating regularly and continually. I encourage staff to come into my office. I repeatedly remind them that my job is to help them be successful; my value to them is in supporting them when they have questions or need help.

I wish I could say that I've always had this much clarity in recognizing my role as a leader. I've always felt a sense of or enjoyed the privilege of being given opportunities to lead. It was only many years through professional development, however, that I also recognized the responsibility. One of the benefits of conducting myself with a confident demeanor is that I'm often given more attention and am provided with more opportunities to lead. That's the privilege; the responsibility is to do it well and to recognize how it impacts those around you and employs those skills in a way that brings everyone up.

I had a lot of energy as a child. Today they might have other labels for my behavior, but it meant that I was challenging myself and often the world around me. For example, all through school, teachers would assign a class project. Invariably, I would approach the teacher after class and say, "I know you asked us to do this project in this way, but what if I explore this other aspect of that idea? Wouldn't that be more interesting? Wouldn't that take us further?" I tended to redesign the class project for myself. It gave me the opportunity to do more. I sought to stretch the limits. Clearly, I was the beneficiary of a nurturing environment. I grew up in communities and in schools that supported that self-exploration; that supported me stretching the boundaries or perhaps breaking the rules. In fifth grade, I burned up a lab table in a science classroom because I created a little experiment to show how you could take dirty water and make it potable. The school was remarkably accommodating given that I melted the top of one of their tables. I've always been the beneficiary of the goodwill and support of teachers and mentors around me. I hope I'm able to pay it back in the way I interact and engage with others.

I credit my family for putting me in those sorts of environments. At the same time, it's taking full advantage of those opportunities and talking to everyone that validates the exposure. It gives me a wonderfully broad perspective of what might be possible. I've been fortunate to come across and work with some brilliant people; with people who have extensive knowledge in specific subjects. I've benefited by taking little kernels away from those interactions and by synthesizing all of those diverse data points into a more holistic perspective of my working model of the world. One strength that has allowed me to be successful in my role as an architect and leader has been my ability to pull up or recapture those data points from a range of industries and often unrelated discussions and apply them to a challenge or a problem in a given circumstance.

I do my best to listen to everyone. I draw inspiration or perspective from anyone I encounter, whether it's on an airplane, in a restaurant or standing in line in a store. While I've not had what might be considered a formal mentor, I'm grateful to the people, including professors and business owners, I think might fall into that category, even if it's in an informal sense. In many cases, I've benefited simply from listening to different people's perspectives, their challenges and their successes; it helps me to modulate my understanding of the world around me.

RANDY VALPY

President and CEO, LifeLearn, Inc.

www.lifelearn.com

Habits are what makes me as a person. They were bred into me as a youngster and have stuck with me and served me very well.

I've had a diverse career — from home furnishings to floor coverings to pet insurance. That seems like a bit of a change, especially since at the time, I did not own a pet and knew nothing about the insurance industry. Then I moved into technology but remained in the animal health industry, so it wasn't as big a switch as going from home furnishings into pet insurance.

I don't have a university education, which was a calculated risk I took back when I was in my early twenties some 30 years ago. My work ethic has, however, undoubtedly played an enormous role in my ability to succeed and take on greater and greater responsibilities. The ability to listen, combined with a very healthy curiosity, has also played a significant role in my success. As a child, we didn't have the technology available to children today, so we were outside all the time and exploring different things. That curiosity has remained with me throughout my life and is the main reason for switching from a substantial career in home furnishings to pet insurance.

When I was headhunted for a pet-insurance role, I hadn't even heard of pet insurance before the call from the headhunter. The more I explored, however, the more research I did, and through that curiosity, I saw such potential for a fantastic industry and business, so I took that leap. Part of my endless interest is asking lots of questions, sometimes to the annoyance of other people, but I'm always asking questions, and that's how I learn a lot.

I'm also very responsive. Typically, whether I get an email from one of my team members at 10 or 10.30 at night, they will get an immediate response from me. That comes from my passion and my love for customer service, which I've had all my life, whether as a newspaper carrier when I was 10 or so, or in my early jobs at McDonald's and other restaurants. Customer service is what differentiates any one company from another.

Procrastination has been a double-edged sword for me. Certainly, when it involves something I'm not anxious to dig into, such as reviewing a 100-page contract, I can quickly find other things to do even though I've got deadlines. Sometimes, however, I get somewhat distracted by the shiny new ball or squirrel. I can be lost in a bit of a rabbit hole at times if I get on to something. Sometimes, though, it pays off well. Other times, I've just wasted half an hour of my life.

I look at those potentially bad habits, but I also think they tie into my curiosity. Sometimes I learn things by procrastinating because I get on to something and see a new product for the company or new service that we can provide. There's work procrastination and home procrastination, which are two entirely different things. I've got a list of things my wife would love me to do but I've been successful in procrastinating for some time. I can't do that at work. Eventually, I've got to face those things that I don't necessarily relish because there are deadlines and other people are relying on me to complete items.

I fly Air Canada exclusively (and I fly a lot with them and have built up 2 million miles so far), and it drives me crazy when they send announcements that they are now charging for this because that's what the other companies are doing. Well, stop being like the others and instead be a market leader! Do something different. It just drives me nuts because being a market leader is what makes a successful company. It's not following in the footsteps of everybody else.

RAJA KHOURY

Co-Founder and President, Pillar Construction

pillarconstruction.com

As a child, I had a great curiosity, and I was interested in many things. Over the years, I developed the habit of consistency and perseverance to go alongside the curiosity. It made me an excellent student, and these habits have intensified since I entered the workforce. Most importantly, I have learned the value of cultivating good habits and of repeating them every day.

I graduated in 1985 from the National School of Public Works, one of the top schools in France. After I finished my undergraduate degree, I went on to get a master's degree in the construction of bridges and tunnels from the same school. In 1986, I came to the United States and did a master's degree in construction management at George Washington University. When I graduated, the economy was not that good, and I had some difficulty finding employment.

My first job was working for a home builder in California. I stayed there for six months, and during that time, I was introduced to a new material for an exterior finish system. I examined the material at length, and I researched the market. No one was selling this product in Washington, D.C., so it seemed an opportune moment to move back and promote the product and achieve a good share of the market. That's how I started my own construction company.

At that time, I had some theoretical ideas but very little experience of what construction meant. Nonetheless, I made my first bid and got my first job six months later. I made a thousand dollars from that contract, and that's how I got into the business. In small part, it was luck, but mostly, it was perseverance. At first, I was alone, but then another engineer, a friend, joined me from California and we started our own company. We chose a new name for the company and continued the business, slowly growing it over the years until it became what it is today.

While the company named Pillar was founded in 1995, the business as such was begun in 1989. Now we have about 300 employees, and we have offices in Houston and New Jersey as well as in the Washington, D.C. area. I find it interesting to look back and see that this all started with just one person and a thousand dollars of profit on a first job.

Over the years, I've tried to maintain a few good habits. One of the most important things for me is how I start my day. I like to wake up early in the morning with a positive attitude. For the last 25 years, my habits have been these: I wake up and get dressed, then I take a walk for half an hour, have coffee, quickly read the newspaper, shower, get dressed again and go to work.

This consistency runs like a thread through both my personal life and my professional life. I have the same friends, and I remain the same, not in what I learn but in terms of energy and perseverance, and I have come to understand that family, friends, co-workers and all those around me rely on these traits. They know that I don't change with every wind that blows. They can count on me to have the same standards and the same principles, and this is reassuring to them.

Whatever changes life brings, I remain steadfast. I awake in a positive frame of mind, determined to do everything I can to ensure the success of my life and my business. I push myself, and I encourage others and sometimes push them to do the same, and I enjoy every moment of it.

I recognize that while the habits of consistency and perseverance have served me well, there is, as with so many good qualities, a downside. Sometimes I push myself too much. Sometimes I push my children, and sometimes I push my employees. There's a fine line between encouraging someone and pushing someone, and I have on occasion crossed it. It can happen first and foremost with me. I become stressed and anxious, and at such moments, I recognize that I need to learn to relax more. So I make a concerted effort to relax and to become more sensitive to the individualized needs of those around me.

I want people to enjoy their lives, and I know that the attitudes and habits I have developed will make them successful and happy. Over time, I've learned that I have to look at other people and see that they don't always see or want the same things that I do. Sometimes it is right to push, but sometimes I have to let people do things their way. I can motivate people, but I cannot change them at the deepest level. Only they can do that.

With time, I've learned to temper my desire to help people, and my judgment has been honed. When we are careful in the exercise of persuasion, our assistance can have a dynamic and positive effect. I see that I have helped many people realize their goals and I've seen how success empowers people.

One of the books that I read lately was introduced to me by my daughter. It is called *Positive*, and it was written by Dr Michael Saag about the AIDS crisis. It's a great book, and I related it closely to my own philosophy, which is to be positive in life. Of course, we have to see the facts and acknowledge what is wrong. We can't go around with the illusion that everything is for the best in the best of all possible worlds, but we have to know also that we have the power to change every moment and make each one favorable. That's the great key to success. Anyone who can do that will live well.

DARREN HILL

Co-Founder and CEO, WebLinc

www.weblinc.com

The times when it was the darkest for our business were the times where we were the most innovative and made the biggest changes that ended up setting us up for success in the future.

I was always somewhat ambitious. I was the kid mowing lawns when I was 10. I earned my cash when I was a kid. As far as optimism goes, however, I had many struggles with reading when I was in elementary school. I have a form of dyslexia, so reading is difficult for me, and school was incredibly difficult for me in those early years. That helped significantly as I learned to smile and work through it, or else I would have been quite miserable. I wasn't a dumb kid; I just learned in a different way. Many adults were, however, telling me I was dumb, and it was an interesting thing as a kid to realize that the adults weren't that smart.

One struggle I have is incorrectly assuming that everybody thinks like I do or wants the same things I want. I'm always having to remind myself that this person isn't me; that they aren't thinking about this problem in the same way that I'm thinking about it. I try to be more understanding of the angle someone could be coming at a problem or situation from. I tend to think, "It's just common sense that I feel this way," and it's not. I feel this way because of all the things that have happened to me in my life, and because someone else has had a completely different set of things influencing them. I try to be conscious about it, but I can fall into the trap of believing my thought to be common sense when it's just my thought, not everybody else's.

Optimism is a habit, and I stay away from bad news to keep it positive. Entrepreneurs have to be optimists, or else we wouldn't take the risks we take. My brother, with whom I started the business, says I have chronic optimism. We get into tough situations, as a company is never perfect. Being able to have a positive outlook and keep muscling through things, making decisions rather than putting my head in the sand, or getting upset about, has worked well for us.

Our industry changes dramatically with each shift. I joke that we've had to start a new business every 18 months as what we were doing in 1994 is wildly different from what we did in 2018. Whenever the company is performing less well than we want, by focusing on the positive aspects of the business, we change the business slightly. We look at the strengths and focus on them. It's a more natural way to say the things we've been working on aren't working, and we can bail on them. We focus on what we do well, and what works.

We took many risks, but they were calculated risks. We've had times when we had to throw everything out that didn't work and keep our core strengths. For instance, before the dot.com bust, many of our clients were dot.com startups. They were venture-backed, and when the venture capital dried up, most of our clients went out of business.

Rather than get down, we focused on the clients who *could* pay their bills, and who *were* doing well, such as the clients we'd done e-commerce projects for who were selling real things to real people. Focusing on them was critical. There were not many companies at that time specifically focused on e-commerce, and providing business-to-business tools to merchants for e-commerce. That was a fantastic move for us.

Any other business person would have shut their company down if they faced what we faced.

Before the bust, we mainly did custom tech projects. We focused on venture-backed startups that had specific ideas of what they needed the technology to do for their startup idea. It was great until it wasn't. It was just amazing, everything we've ever read about the dot.com era and money was flying around. It was just awesome. Within a three-week period, it went from awesome to not being viable anymore.

For our industry, it was way worse than the financial recession of 2008. It was catastrophic, as most of the companies we worked with went out of business. That was a tough time, but I'm so glad we made the changes we made at that time as we would have never made it otherwise. It set us up for success.

Aside from chronic optimism, I work hard. I know I've got a limited amount of time in the day, in the week, in my life, and I want to be able to get things done and prioritize those. Knowing how to prioritize comes from knowing that you can't get it all done. Anyone that thinks they're fantastic at multitasking is lying to themselves, or somebody on his or her team isn't telling them the truth.

I learned how to prioritize by being highly focused on making sure that I'm getting the most important things done first. Another one that goes with it is email. I set aside time in the morning, and then time at the end of the day to go through email, and it's rare for me to have more than ten unread messages in my inbox. That helps me prioritize as well; to make sure I'm paying attention to the right things. I make sure that I respond to everyone that I need to respond to at specific hours of the day.

JOAN WELLS

CEO and Co-Founder, Wellington

wellingtonexperience.com

The habit of journaling has been good because it helps me focus on the important things. It gives me a better perspective, and it also gives me better insight into what I'm thinking and what other people are thinking.

My biggest habit is I never say, "No". That can be a good thing, and it can be a bad thing. If someone calls me and asks, "Is now a good time?", I always say, "Yes". If someone stops by my office and asks, "Do you have a minute?", I always say "Yes". Then it's midnight, and I haven't checked my email once, so I've had to make a schedule. What I've done is take 8 to 10 a.m. every day and made that my planning time; my working, thinking and emailing time. I make that my block. I start the day with that, and it's not something that looms over me all day long. Then it's a freeing experience because I can immerse myself in meetings or interactions with people because I have cleared my virtual desk.

I'm boring. I make the same smoothie every single day. It's crazy and highly complicated, and I'm convinced that I have to have this smoothie every day of my life. I have to start my day with that, and I drink four cups of coffee.

Additionally, I keep two journals that I run at one time — a personal journal and a professional one. They're separate for a reason, because even though I'm the same person professionally as I am personally, sometimes I can't sort through the emotions of what I'm feeling at the time. Am I concerned about something professionally or personally? Am I tired because I'm depleting myself professionally or personally? They are two different states of being. So I journal both personally and professionally with those two different books. My books go back to 2008 when I started this habit. It's great to go back and read through the things that I was worried about back then. Now I can laugh and realize it was nothing to be concerned about. Most things tend to work themselves out. We go through different phases in life, and it's neat to have that written documentation of our experiences.

I discern solutions to problems or make decisions through journaling and introspection. I also read many books on meditation, and I'm a prayerful person. So I combine all of those habits along with writing, and that's played an enormous role in who I am as a person, both personally and professionally.

I try to get it done in that morning block while I'm drinking the smoothie and the four cups of coffee. Usually, while I'm doing that, I'm planning my day. My habits have been successful because the older I get, I see that they have given me a good perspective.

Additionally, I try to exercise every day. I take 17 vitamins, and I make my smoothie. I've learned that I have to take care of myself because I've depleted my health at many times throughout my life, feeling that I didn't have control over my health because my job was never done. As an entrepreneur, there's always more I can be doing. I've realized that I have to be my best self, and figure out how to be my best self to give to others.

ROB CASTIGLIONE

Partner, WNY Asset Management

www.wnyasset.com

My habits play a large part in my success; however, I didn't learn these successful habits till later in life — organization, communication, discipline and learning from failure.

I learned to organize, communicate, and be more self-disciplined over the years. Sometimes I wish I had learned earlier, but I don't have regrets, and everything has fallen into line.

I've looked to learn from failure. For example, I'm a Type A personality, and my partners are not. Most of the environment around me is not what would be considered Type A. This, of course, is not a 'failure' on anyone's part, but it did require that I first recognize that environment and then adapt to it and to those around me. I've learned to cultivate the habit of recognizing an environment and adjusting my approach. It's no different from dealing with my sons and needing to correct them on something; I have to make sure I have the right approach.

I'm results-oriented, so ideally I would like to say something short and to the point and have those around me get it and execute. When working with others, however, I've learned to recognize when my environment requires more of a coaching or development role from me. Am I perfect at that execution all the time? No. I am, however, always improving on my habits.

I had to learn to understand how different approaches are. Sometimes you can get to the same answer by going in different directions, so I recognize that mine isn't always the best one, and I'm okay with that. Part of being successful is the ability to continue evolving and learning. If we're not changing and learning, that could be dangerous in a particular environment as things continue to progress across all fields. We could get left behind.

I've also learned to recognize when not to fight what I'm truly meant to do. I focus on areas in which I excel as we're not designed to do all things equally well. I ask myself what my strengths are. Part of being good at what I bring to the table in an entrepreneurial space is being able to recognize and focus on my proficiencies.

For my weaker skills, I have a team around me. If I didn't have that type of a think tank, I could lock myself in an office and convince myself that I'm right all day long. It's essential to have a team and perhaps a little business paranoia. I ask myself continually if my team and I are getting better, and I look for ways where we can improve.

In our business, we know who we are and who we serve. We know that we cannot service all clients correctly. I have to be careful as an entrepreneur to adhere to the knowledge of who I am, what I'm meant to do, and who I can serve.

It's great to support and to dream, as the mind is a wonderful thing, but there is also reality. There are no rules when you dream; it's the time to imagine and the time to create. We also have to be honest with ourselves. What are we intended for? Where do we excel? We have to be okay with what we're designed to do and not fight it. It took me years to realize that I was fighting myself. Once I embraced what I believe I was meant to do, that's when my career started to feel complete and I began to feel fulfilled.

RON HORNING

Owner, RJ Technologies
www.rjtechnologies.com

What's nice about working out is if I need to, I can take out my frustrations on weights or cardio machines.

I've had a workout routine for many years. As a habit, diligence is essential. If we want to build muscle or lose weight, it doesn't happen overnight; it takes time. In working with clients, we have to come to that realization as well, especially when we go out and propose a new project. We have to understand that it's not going to happen overnight. It takes time to build that rapport and relationship and understanding from both sides to make it work.

As a child, I saw that things didn't always come quickly, and it took time to get things done. Throughout the years, as I gained more experience, I only saw more of that. Definitely, in the corporate world, I saw how long it took to accomplish things. Say I need to get a project going, yet it takes a long time for corporate to turn that around and get the ball rolling. When starting the business, I strove to be mindful of that and continually reminded myself that it wasn't going to happen on Day 1. I wasn't fearful, as I knew that it usually would turn around and come out if it was the right thing.

One of the big things we need to watch out for is multitasking. We all get involved with multitasking too much. We're working on one thing, and another idea pops in our heads, and then we say, "Oh, that's right. I have to work on that other thing too."We jump over to the other thing and work on that, and then we forget what we were initially doing. Then we go to shut down the computer at night and see that email that we were drafting earlier in the day and realize we forgot all about it.

We all do this nowadays, and I'm trying to pull back on that habit. I believe there are scientific studies that say the brain was not built to multitask. It was made to do one thing at a time, and we're just driving ourselves crazy by trying to do so many things at the same time. It takes longer to get those things done because we multitask. It's hard these days, though, because there are so many things on the plate, and something triggers it, and we jump over to that, so we don't forget it.

Patience and investing time is the key.

RAY GREEN

Co-Founder, Paradigm Learning, Inc.

paradigmlearning.com

To be successful in sales, I have to have a process.

I usually don't go to bed until around 11 or 12 , but I'm always up at 7 in the morning. It takes me about 10 minutes to do back workouts, then I eat breakfast, and get to my morning habits. I usually work out in the garden, and I work out with a trainer once a week at his location. So I do a little bit of exercise, and I work in the garden for a couple of hours, and I play golf a couple of afternoons per week.

I retired from day-to-day operations in 2008 and now work on the business with my senior management team, rather than in the business, so naturally I have habits around my company as well. I speak with my CFO and controller on Tuesday mornings when we review cash flow and accounts receivable. We discuss any issues, what we need to do and how that piece of our business operates. My Friday morning session is with the chief operating officer, and we look at operations and sales opportunities, and address any problems or concerns.

One of my habits is always looking at what needs to be done, who needs to do it and getting it done. We attack business situations from that set of practices. We have a discipline to the process, so we repeat that process over and over again. We'll draft something to break it down. We break it down as quickly as we can so it doesn't stay on our plate any longer than it has to. If we're going to get it done, we get it done as quickly as we can.

Sales is a process, and we have to know how to do it. In the early days of selling, I learned the discipline to the process, and that's helped me a lot. As a child, I was more of a daydreamer, and I would find myself helicoptering up as a habit; looking over the big picture of what was going on in my little world. I tend to helicopter up now and look at the big picture and where we fit into our business space. We also have to realize what's going on in all of our client's worlds so we can fit into that and help them manage their businesses — because that's what we get paid to do.

One of the things I had to modify is when I thought it was time to bring someone new into our business. It was time to let a new set of eyes see the company from the way we'd been running it and let them do it and support them in doing so. We brought in people who didn't understand our business, and we recruited them hard. We thought we'd done the best job we could in sorting out the right people, but we realized that we had the wrong people.

They'd put in a new system of demand-generation operation as opposed to having salespeople on the street in front of our clients — and it was killing our business. I talked to my cousin's husband who's in charge of an $80,000,000 company. I asked him what he did with his time as he's in his family's 130-year-old textile business. He said, "I'm in front of customers all the time. If you're not in front of your customers, your business will dry up."

I saw that we had this demand-generation marketing and were not in front of our customers like we used to be. That was a mistake, and we had to disassemble that, take it apart, and go back to doing what we knew how to do, and it worked.

We almost broke it, however, and it was a painful lesson. It probably took about 18 months to figure out that it was not going in the direction it needed to go. We got it done, but it's taken nearly two years to unravel it. In the end, it turned out fine because we caught it in time.

Most importantly, consistency has been the No.1 successful habit. For example, when we first started the company, we established relationships with our most important partners, such as our attorneys, bankers, auditors and accountants. We still have relationships with them all, as they have been critical partners in helping us accomplish what we want to achieve.

To summarize, I feel it's important to surround myself with others who are stronger where I'm weak. My own weakness has been having poor attention to detail in some operational areas of the business, such as in marketing and product development. My strength is providing the vision and strategic objectives, so I've needed to count on other people to execute that vision and meet those objectives. Recognizing and admitting weaknesses and finding ways to compensate for those is key to leadership success.

PART FOUR

NEGATIVE HABITS

Positive habits make supreme leaders. The reality, however, is that all of us, no matter how long we've been in business, or how successful we are, have experienced failures and setbacks.

We all have what we can refer to as negative habits. Maybe we still wrestle with them at present. Perhaps they were influential earlier in our career and our lives. They could have held us back from even greater success, or caused significant problems.

We noticed that while our leaders had negative habits, they also had the practice of managing them to obtain a better outcome. It could be that they hired others in their companies to compensate for their weaknesses. Some leaders used what was once a harmful habit and turned it into a strength.

JOE CARBERRY

Executive Officer, Medical Solutions Supplier

www.medsolsupplier.com

A fire put out is a fire put off.

One practice that has contributed to my success is to keep questioning my decision-making process. Many people with great ideas believe in them wholeheartedly and go 100 percent straightforward. They may not have the proper balance of strategically thinking things through, evaluating whether or not there are external factors to impede those ideas, or considering the possible repercussions of their decisions.

I always try to look at every possible outcome — whether it's good, bad or indifferent — to determine whether decisions made are the right ones. Decisions are made one of two ways — through gut feeling or by detailed analysis of a situation. I combine the two.

This habit of self-doubt has shaped the direction of our organization. I always believed that I wasn't the smartest person in the room and that I had to gain information from everybody else around me to make the proper decision. Somewhere in the middle is a happy balance that's called informed intuition.

I always doubt my initial thought process until I get to a place where my gut lines up with the knowledge I've gained. Then I feel informed enough to make those decisions. A firefighter in California recently gave an interview and said, "A fire put out is a fire put off." He said the answer to firefighting is not becoming better at putting forest fires out; it's developing communities and buildings and homes and roadways that are fire-resistant.

Entrepreneurs can fall into the trap of continually putting out fires rather than preventing them in the first place. The key to success is building a company that's fireproof. This allows all that happens around us to ebb and flow while we remain secure. This concept completely changed my mind about the way our leadership team handles situations and troubleshoots internal and external business issues.

When I spend more time focusing on my weaknesses and try to improve upon them, the more mediocre I become because I'm not living in my strengths. In other words, many things aren't my forte. The more I try to get better at them, the less time is spent allowing my strengths to thrive.

That plays out in every area of life, no matter what the role is. The more I've chosen to live in my strengths while allowing my weaknesses to be overcome by the strengths of others, the more effective I've become.

I can't take credit for this concept; there's a great book called *The Freak Factor* by David J. Rendall. In our company, we use this book as a guidepost to conduct performance reviews. Rather than look at what our team members accomplished or didn't accomplish, we look at their strengths and their weaknesses. We encourage them to delegate activities that fall under their weaknesses and to take ownership of the ones that rely on their strengths.

For example, one of the things that I've learned over the last two years is that ideas and thoughts can't be captive to time; they happen when they happen. As a leader, it's my responsibility to have a good idea, capture those thoughts and then process those thoughts. The processing of those thoughts happens at the same time every day.

When ideas happen, I take screenshots to capture them, and then, every morning at 9, the service I use emails me every screenshot that I captured from the day before. I designate time in the morning to take all those ideas and process them. I sort them first by asking is it something I need to work on; is it something I need to share with a team member; is it something I need to schedule time in the future to dig into.

That's how I focus on my strengths, keep our company fireproof, and use my habits to benefit those around me.

SETH EARLEY

CEO, Earley Information Science

www.earley.com

I like to say that I failed my way to success because I didn't give up and instead I kept trying.

Some people talk about eating the frog first, as in if you had to eat a frog every day, you would want to eat it first thing in the morning. Well, I eat my frogs later in the day or in the evening; that's my peak frog-eating time. It's also a matter of choosing to evaluate how I spend my time. Am I going to watch TV and hang out or read a book? Am I going to work on one of the problems that I need to solve or work on some aspect of the business?

It's a matter of focusing my time and energy on the things that are important and not just the things that are urgent. The difference is that something can be urgent but not important, or important but not critical. It's a matter of asking what's the critical thing I need to do. I look at that rather than looking at what's making noise or seems to be the thing to do at that moment but perhaps is not the best use of my time.

One of the things that we've done over the years to stand out as a small professional services firm is to do research and share our thinking to produce thought leadership in our space. That means we spend much time doing research, learning, and producing an output to write an article or a white paper, or put together a webinar or a workshop to share knowledge.

Those are things that can easily be pushed off or deprioritized because they don't seem to provide any short-term value; however, the long-term benefit is significant. Many times, when I'm working on a project, that project will not come to fruition for a couple of months. I must realize that there are things that I need to do today that are not going to produce an immediate value but will deliver value down the road.

Having that longer-term mindset about the things that I spend my time on is essential. It's like work. It's like exercise. I'm no longer a kid, but I try to work out regularly to maintain my physical health, and I'm in quite good shape. I've worked at it for years and years, and there are parts of the business that I've also worked at for years and years.

It does take time to see results, but we do see results. It's having that long-term mindset and engaging in the day to day habits and activities that cannot help but pay off. I don't always see the progress, and I don't always know the value, and keeping that long-term perspective in mind while doing things in a short-term way may not necessarily have any pay right away. That's been an essential part of our success over the years.

Different types of habits can produce results in different ways at different points in life and in business. For example, one of my habits is perseverance and not giving up until I achieve something. Sometimes, however, there's a significant obstacle. It's not trivial, but it may not be something that can be overcome. Continuing to fight the battle and to persevere in the face of an obstacle that was not going to go away does me a disservice. It's not an appropriate use of time and energy.

The things that made me successful as an entrepreneur stopped serving me at a certain point. There are times when I have to realize that it's hard for a reason. Maybe I'm not doing it correctly and putting in more energy and focus and time is not going to help. Sometimes I have to take a step back and ask if I'm doing the right thing. Am I just putting in the effort because this is what I'm used to?

The other habit that I've had over the years that has not served me well is always looking for a problem, the downside, the gap or what's not working. That does work to a certain degree, and it may be a good thing to do if it's just me working. My habit of looking for the gap or the problem or the issue or the thing that's not being done correctly does not help when working with a team of people where perfection is the enemy of good; it can be demotivating.

The other habit I've had over the years is always assuming that I wasn't quite getting things right and that I had something to learn no matter the situation. Because I invented everything I'm doing, most of the time I was making mistakes and I would keep trying and keep going to succeed. A *mea culpa* attitude can be a tremendous disservice to me and to my organization.

I had to stop thinking about continually improving, and to start thinking about what is. Because my expectations for myself and the people around me were high, even when we didn't do a very good job, we did a good job. Even when in my mind it wasn't what it should have been or could have been, it was a lot better than almost anything else that we would encounter. It doesn't serve me to fall on my sword or miss perfection when my good is better than most people's excellent.

JOHN M. HUMPHREY

President and CEO, July Services

www.julyservices.com

One of the top characteristics of success is to get in touch with my strengths and weaknesses.

Looking back, I can see many keys that I feel were important to my success. One would be surrounding myself with quality people, and concerning the types of people, we like to identify them as those with a sense of urgency and those who take high initiative. We recognize that every individual is different and contributes differently, and it's vital for us to build on strengths with individuals. Building on strengths and empowering people to leverage their strengths in the organization is important. So the first thing is to develop a reliable team of individuals that leverage their strengths.

Second is being disciplined to a work ethic. There's a lot to be said for getting up every day and going to work at the same time and putting in a hard day's work. I've found that over the years, there's no perfection in achieving success in anything. Some of the best things that happen are often the failures because I look back and see, learn, and grow. What allows me to overcome those obstacles is the persistence and commitment to a discipline of coming into work every day.

A third thing is defining my purpose and values. From the outset, we should work with the team to develop and identify core values. We did that late in our business model, and while we always had core values and we had an idea where we were going and what the directions were, we didn't have it written down, and we didn't think through it in detail. It's important to establish core values, a mission and a vision for the organization; to work with key team members to establish that right from the first day because those are essential to keeping the business moving in the right direction and ensuring that everyone's on the right page.

Every person has a downside, and often there's a flip side to that strength, and I'm no different. There are several parts of my personality that I've learned to mute. I surround myself with others to fill some gaps, and I would say that's an important thing for young entrepreneurs to do.

For example, I have a strong personality, and I'm a passionate person. I didn't recognize that that passion often was overshadowing and overpowering others to provide input. I didn't see that until later in my career, and I didn't understand that. For me, it's important to get in touch quickly with that side of my personality and not be the one at the meeting who's always speaking, but to be asking questions and encouraging others to provide input.

I'm open to ideas. I love debating different perspectives on an issue, and I like poking on whether we could go this way or that way. We need to do that, but for people like me who like ideas, it's important to be surrounded by a good decision-making team to make good decisions and stay the course. Because sometimes I might fall in love with my idea when it may not necessarily be the best idea, I had to work on surrounding myself with good people to help check me a bit.

For budding entrepreneurs, discipline is essential and having a plan is important too. One of the things that we did later in our business model was put together a robust process for guiding our strategic initiatives and plans every year. That's a team effort, and it helps my team have clarity on what we're going to do and what we're not going to do. Entrepreneurs need to make sure that they have a good process for what it is they're working on to focus on the essential items.

JIM SALTER

CEO and Shareholder, Infinity Contractors

www.infinitycontractors.com

I feel like I've got a Ph.D. in things that are messed up, because I've messed up a lot. I have, however, learned a lot from them. I make each mistake only once.

The way I developed was I got myself into trouble on a few projects. I had to figure out how to solve problems. By getting myself into trouble, I've learned more from making mistakes than I have from any class I've ever sat in before. It's through the hard knocks in life that I've received most of my education.

Early on in the building trades, I wasn't experienced enough to understand that. As I developed, however, I started realizing that I had to find a better way to get something done. The piecemeal approach to solving a problem grew out of making mistakes of my own.

The best thing that'll teach someone something is to lose a bunch of money. I tell my employees that I don't have a problem with them making a mistake once. If they make the mistake a second time, soon after they've made that mistake, I've got a problem with that, because they didn't learn from the error. We should all learn from mistakes because that's what makes us better at what we do.

If someone takes his own money and goes to a casino and puts down a thousand dollars on black on a roulette wheel, and it comes up red, he learns not to put a thousand dollars down on a 50-50 chance. When something costs me personally, whether it's through time, emotional tolls on me or financial tolls, I learn something from it.

When my mind is occupied with problems, it's hard to move forward. I become stagnant trying to solve the problems. I'm in a bad place. It's like being in a cave with no lights. I can't figure anything else out until I get some light. I've got to find that way to solve those problems. Moreover, if I'm in the dark emotionally, I'm not going to be moving forward.

I developed a feel because I've been in a lot of difficult situations in my life, but I've always tried to look at the big picture. I might not be able to solve that problem right now, but in two weeks I can solve it. I might have to take some lumps between now and that two-week period, but I'll win in the end. For example, when I started my business, I worked seven days a week, sunup to sundown, and sometimes, many hours after sunset. I put everything back into my business for the first five years, and then my payday came.

I had a plan to wait. Emotionally, many people want to get what they want now. By me being disciplined enough to wait, it put me in a better position in the market, and I was able to grow the company a lot better. I rolled the money back into it. So, it wasn't about me getting on top of it right away; it was about being successful first.

I didn't go to college until I was 44. I got my son out of college, and he became a mechanical engineer in May 2000. In August 2000, I got into graduate school, skipping a bachelor's degree by testing and interviewing through the process. I went through the Neeley School of Business in Fort Worth, and got a master's in business administration. It was something that I'd always wanted to do.

My son asked, "Pop, why do you need to go to college? You've done okay for yourself." I told him that I'd wondered my whole life what I could have done had I gone to college and had a degree. Being the oldest of six children, there wasn't money to send me to school. We didn't know anything about grants. No one in my family had ever been to college. So I went to a trade school instead.

I'd always wondered what if. Once I figured out that I could apply, I called and asked the folks if they ever took anyone with life experience. When I was told they did, I wondered if the gal was being nice to me. I applied, though, and was selected. I remember the first day when everybody stood up and talked about what his or her history had been. For some people, this was their second postgraduate degree. Some folks had a master's degree in chemical engineering, professional certifications, all kinds of qualifications. When it got to me, I told them I had a master's degree in sewer-ology. I was kidding around a little because I was a master plumber, so I threw that out there. When they realized what I was saying, the class got a laugh out of it.

As I went through my first semester, I had never studied at that level before in my life. I was a deep reader, which made me a slow reader. At the end of the first semester, I said to my son, "Your pop might have bitten off more than he can chew in this deal."

He said, "Dad, you always wanted to do that. Stay with it. We'll pick up the slack at the office."

So I just dug into it and got my head back into the game, and figured out how to read with a highlighter. When I got out, I had a 3.3 GPA, which felt good, considering where I had come from to get onto a master's program. I would walk out of the classroom and put the stuff to work in my business the next day because this stuff was all for me.

Lastly, I've learned that if I help other people get what they want, I'll also get what I want. It'll come to me every time. It took me many years to figure that out, but once I put my employees in a position in which they could share in the wins of the company, I learned that if they were winning, I didn't have to worry about me. I would be winning. Because if they're on top of it, I will be automatically.

JEROME HENIN

Owner and President, Henin Realty

heninrealty.com

It's a habit that I have to keep re-evaluating everything.

I used to be a single father, so I raised my son and grew the companies on the two continents. I was extremely precise in what I was doing, so I have a routine. Maybe it's boring, but it's fairly predictable how things go every morning, even to the point where my daughter knows exactly what to expect.

I'm very much a person of principle. I wouldn't say I like to deviate from my core values, even if sometimes they are not high-fashion values. For instance, not putting myself in danger in my business is not an obvious thing, because most people are quickly overextending themselves, or they do things, and they forget about values. One of my habits is to stick to strong, solid values.

I'm much into staying within patterns of not believing what my systems are telling me or even what my gut is telling me. My habit is to wait things out and to be open-minded.

I don't take anything for granted. I don't believe that things will simply happen because we press certain buttons, or follow specific rules. For instance, I have a strong behavior in that I don't trust anyone easily. I was young, and when I started, people were approaching me saying that I had to give capital trust to people. I always did the opposite. I don't trust anyone or anything. I will find out and make my judgment, but I don't give capital trust to people. I have a habit of being cautious.

I do take tremendous risks, and I like to lead to different things that have never happened before, but it has to be on my terms. I have faith in me more than in other people. One of the habits is to follow my guts, my feelings and my enthusiasm. I tend to be in tune with every aspect of everything we do. I have a habit to micromanage, as I like to be able to get into anything that goes on immediately. I want to know what's going on with my business. I get involved and go into details with people; not that I need to, but I care. Even though I have a CFO, a bookkeeper and an accountant, I'm always logging in and checking everything.

The biggest thing I've modified along the years is to be patient. I'm quick, and I tend to believe that people know what I'm talking about because they can read my mind. Many people look at me, and they wonder which subject it is now because I switch. I'm learning, and I'm continually trying to be more disciplined in being slower, and more patient, and not assume that everybody's on the same page.

For instance, I remember that when I used to work for a huge company, I'd wonder how come they couldn't agree to buy some land, or do a project, or do my ideas. I wasn't in charge. At that time, I learned that we put it on the side, we sit on it, we re-evaluate, and we come back later. I was so frustrated. I gradually came to learn, however, the benefit of acting in this way. Despite my mind sometimes jumping left and right, and wanting to go in this or that direction, now I'm trying to slow down and get back to the explanation of things, and sometimes sit on something, and wait it out.

This has created a new habit — I never panic. There's no fire here. Don't worry about it. We'll deal with it. We can afford it. We know what to do. That has been a big difference. It's dramatically changed my way of acting and behaving; my habit of striking, quick, moving, boom, straight, and not letting anybody talk. Now it's like the opposite.

DEB BEAIRD

Principal and Executive Consultant, Beaird Group

www.beairdgroup.com

Multitasking can be both a positive habit and a negative one.

I probably get out of bed a little too enthusiastically, which can be abrupt for other people. I brush my teeth, shower, dress, start coffee, make the bed, and then make breakfast.

I have breakfast with my husband. An essential habit is having breakfast and dinner as a family. It does get broken occasionally, but that's perhaps the most important habit. The other habits that have played a role in my success are servant leadership, showing generosity and kindness.

Most of my habits have been in place since childhood. Even as a teenager, I was involved with various organizations and developing leadership skills across groups, whether it was through girl scouts, sport, yearbook, Model United Nations or Swim Guard. It was by working with lots of interesting people and disparate groups and developing skills along the way that I developed the ability to do more than one thing at a time. I've had to modify my habit of multitasking. I've learned to make sure that when I'm working with people, I'm focused on one thing at a time and we're entirely conscious of each other, and that I'm not trying to do more than one thing.

In terms of the success of the business, some of the practices that have contributed to the growth and the tenure of our team have been a combination of servant leadership, serving the people who are on our team, and generosity and kindness. I don't tolerate people being inappropriately unkind. I value listening and respecting the entire team for their ideas, being inclusive, open-minded and learning from others. I see the importance of empowering others. If somebody has accepted a position to do something, let her do it. It may not be the way I'd do it, but it's going to get done, and that contributes to the growth of the business.

GARY NICHOLS

CEO and President, Revel Architecture and Design

revelers.com

Don't keep fumbling with email. Look at it, take care of it, deal with it. Delete it, file it, or act on it, because it just sits in the rinse cycle. It just keeps tumbling.

One good habit to have is to be efficient with information. I'm an information broker. I know it sounds a little odd, but that's what I do. The more experience I get, the more knowledge that I have to share, so people are coming to me to get information, whether it's a budget or a schedule or advice or whatever.

I'm able to disseminate information freely and rapidly. I have to make myself available so people will want to come to get information from me because that's the best thing to have happen for success. If I'm too busy and I can't talk at a particular time, people aren't going to come up to me and ask me for the information that they need that I have inside me.

I'm the broker of this information, so I make myself available, even though it's difficult to multitask in that form because I'm having to do my work while people are just extemporaneously coming up to me and saying, "Hey, what about this?" I try to look at it quickly and answer it, and I teach people that when they come up to ask me for information, I've got all the information that I need to answer the question. Being available to answer questions has been a success story for me. It's hard to do, though, because I can't get my work done, because I have my tasks sitting in front of me.

I trust my instincts completely. There have been numerous times when I sensed that something was starting to go a little sideways, and sure enough, it was. Trusting my instincts is critical. Our instincts are there for a reason, so if we trust them and listen to them, that's a great habit to have.

I make the business a bit of a game so that I enjoy it. Even at the beginning of my career, when I was working on some of the not-so-pleasant stuff, I would grind it out. I made the unsavory parts of the work more interesting by seeing how fast I could get them done. If I could get them done quickly, they wouldn't be sitting there, and I wouldn't be trudging through the mud. I'd skip over the mud quickly, so I made it a game. I still do that.

Worrying is one thing I have to control so I don't worry myself sick, because it's easy to do that. I have to manage my psyche even if it's difficult to do. Having 45 people to feed, in our industry, it's feast or famine. It's not regular. Suddenly, we could have a huge campus to work on, and it could stop and all of a sudden, those six people don't have any work. The no-worrying part is also a habit that's important; to know that things will work themselves out eventually.

I procrastinate. I'm not too fond of paperwork and never have been. I get people that help me, and then I have made paperwork a bit of a game, knowing that if I get it done, it's all set and I can get the contract signed, and it's solid.

I'm a people person, so I don't particularly like confrontation.

I will avoid it, which is dangerous because human resources issues come up and I have to deal with them. I've learned not to take it into myself and to keep it outside of myself. I can sit down with somebody and be honest. It always works itself out, but as I approach it as a human being, I could worry and think, "Oh, this is going to be so uncomfortable and so sticky." It's worse if I put it off and don't deal with it.

Many of us play ostrich. We want the problem to go away, so we hope that if we stick our head in the sand, it's going to go away. It took me about ten years to figure out that that was a negative habit. I would think, "Ooh! I don't want to mess that up. It's going to go away. Please go away. Please go away." It never goes away. That's a negative habit that I had that I learned finally to overcome and just hit it because unfortunately, it's never going to go away.

BOB MOORE

Founder, Infotech Resources

itresources.com

When I'm starting something, I don't know what I don't know, so I'm learning as I'm going.

We create habits based on behaviors that we want to support. For example, I always try to work out in the morning. I have to keep my mind and body in sync, particularly as I get older. It's important to take time to keep myself in shape. When I was younger, I was more of a night owl. I tend to get up earlier now, so I try to start the day at least three or four times a week with exercising.

I don't stay up as late as I used to. When we're single and in college, we tend to stay up late, get up and muffle our way through class, and go to work afterward. It's naturally a late type of world that students are in. As I get older, I realize that I have to get up and be on time, and I should preferably be a little early to work, and get things done, and be able to get a hold of people.

If I exercise in the morning, I feel sharper all day long. I don't need that extra cup of coffee, and I'm able to go hard for that nine or ten hours a day that I'm working. By the time I leave the office, it's usually between 6 and 7 o'clock at night. Going over to the gym to spend an hour and a half there and not getting home until 8.30 doesn't work for me.

When I was younger, I paid my way through school. I started working at a young age because of our family situation. My dad retired when I was in sixth grade, and my mom was a beautician, so there wasn't a whole lot of extra income coming in. If I wanted to have any extra money, I always had to work.

I got a paper route as soon as I was eligible, but before that I came up with other ideas for making money. I held carnivals at the weekend in the neighborhood or asked to wash somebody's car. I was always responsible for taking the initiative, and trying to figure out ways of doing things and ways I could make money so that I could do the things that I wanted to do.

As time went on, one of the things that maybe held me back was that my objective with the business was always to be profitable. I wasn't going to go into a bunch of debt, but I started the company, and I was making good money in software sales. To stay profitable, I didn't invest as much into the business. Now that it has been profitable, I feel I didn't push the envelope. That's a habit that I've probably been getting out of recently because we're spending a lot more money on the business itself these days than I was initially.

My objectives changed a bit more. I don't need to maximize profitability. I'm a little bit more focused on growth. I'm going to focus more on hiring as many people as I can. I put away that habit of insisting on doing nothing that's going to disrupt that profitability. In the past, I did more things on my own, and now I'm hiring people to do the things that I always tended to be in charge of myself. That's a different approach to doing things and a different habit that I've got to adhere to now.

One of my habits is to keep 'sharpening the saw'. I was always reading and trying to figure out better ways to improve myself. At 22, coming out of college, how could I get better? It's surprising to me how few people do that; they go about their day, and don't worry about making themselves better and more effective. That's something that I always try to preach to people here; I say, "Hey, keep sharpening the saw."

I don't know if I would have changed anything about my path because I learned from everything I did. Perhaps I would have been a little bit more aggressive in building up the company sooner rather than later. Expanding and growing and getting into other areas, I went after a few markets that didn't make as much sense in retrospect, but I wouldn't say that was a mistake. It was all part of the learning curve.

DAVID MAVASHEV

CEO, Nastel
www.nastel.com

I always anticipate potential situations. I hope for the best, but I'm continuously prepared for a setback and I'm able to handle that setback.

I was born in the Soviet Union. There they taught us to keep our word, to be honest, and do our homework on time, and do whatever we have to do to prepare for our exams. We were also to be good friends and good to our parents.

The approach was also that there was no ability to be an entrepreneur. I studied math, but I also wanted to be a scientist. In everything I did, I wanted to excel. I'm not sure if it's a habit, but the fact is that the desire to make a difference led to certain successful endeavors and continued to drive me.

When I started the company, I had a specific vision. I was in a unique position and had the habit to learn and to understand the actual needs of the company and create something of a difference. That was more of a drive in me. I became educated about what the customer and the market needed.

I didn't have any external investors to drive the actual vision. It was more the ability to succeed and make a difference against companies that had a lot of resources and capital. Our competitors when we were a startup were multibillion-dollar companies, so it was fighting like David against Goliath.

The desire to win, combined with my drive to demonstrate what I could do to make a difference in the marketplace and not being afraid of big companies with many resources, was the driving force behind my success. We could convince the actual customer to choose us instead of a giant. At some point, it was not relevant, but at the beginning it was relevant.

We had agility, a vision of the future, help for customer needs and were on the level of assisting them to understand that we're not just here to sell, but here to help. That's the significant difference by which they actually can see that we can help them to reach their goals, not only for this specific area but where they want to end up in several years.

Many mistakes happened, however. It was my horror school. Once when we were supposed to exit, we didn't listen to our feelings but to those of others. That caused the mistake of us not taking a lucrative offer. Going through this learning curve probably cost us millions of dollars.

We weathered different types of recessions in 2001 and 2008. Despite those mistakes that happened through the entire duration of running the company, we continued to grow and continued to remain profitable. We could have been in a better position.

Some people in the company become sloppy, and sloppiness is unacceptable because sloppiness can cost a company millions of dollars. We found when going through that exercise that some people caused that and they were let go. That's why it's important to be able to choose the right people for the business, otherwise sloppy situations can happen. I learned it's essential in business to have the right people.

We must be cautious in our decisions and take calculated risks. One of the important things is not to be a gambler. Some people get lucky but we have to make calculated decisions and be ready to handle potential failures so we don't go drastically down. Some companies who don't handle things properly disappear.

LAWRENCE JOSS

CEO, Surfaces USA

surfacesusa.com

I have a lot of negative habits. I just have a couple of positive habits more than negative habits, but I'm always correcting my behavior.

For much of my early days in business, I had a lot of loyal and hardworking people working for me, and I was all about myself. I was self-centered and narcissistic, and all the money that I was making — along with everything else — was about me. It wasn't about sharing and it wasn't about thinking outside of my privilege. I'm coming to terms with that now, especially as opening up the way the company and its culture could change through making changes in myself has been important.

At the beginning of my career, I wasn't often honest. I was under-capitalized, so I strung out suppliers. I did whatever it took to be successful at anyone's expense. I was just so self-centered. The biggest change I've made is to stop thinking about myself all the time.

That pivot shrank my business footprint. Instead of chasing the money, the consumerism and the next rush, I've been able to increase the quality of my life, and that of the people around me. The game has changed from consumption to inclusion in trying to create a happier environment.

13 years ago, I got sober, and my marriage fell apart. My whole life crumbled in on itself. From that point, I had to

re-evaluate who I was as a human being and what I wanted in my life. I started a regular meditation practice, and my life changed from a small, narrow-minded, self-centered focus to a more global focus. I found myself wanting to be of service.

It's a lot of work, and I show up every day. I'm a seeker, and I ask many questions, and I show up at random places to keep working and expanding. It keeps changing who I am as an entrepreneur; even the idea of what an entrepreneur can be is changing so drastically for me. I embrace the great opportunity to be of service and help other people instead of just helping myself.

There's something remarkably intimate in being an entrepreneur. It's about hunger and a desire to get from Point A to Point B and figuring out how to do that while not necessarily having the template. It's about showing up every day and trying — and about being okay with failing. That's one of the things that I've done; just as much as I've succeeded, I've failed. I've just happened to succeed a few more times than I failed.

Creativity is an important facet of being an entrepreneur. It's about not being stuck in a place of preconceptions, thinking that we know what a business looks like. It may be about reinventing a business over and over again. I would say the most critical skill that I have as an entrepreneur is that I'm a good listener and I ask many questions. I don't need my voice to be heard so people can listen to my story. I'm interested in getting information and learning, and that gives me an advantage over most people.

I'm an evolution of my curiosity. When I was young, I didn't care about anyone. The only person I cared about was me. As

I've grown and matured, it's become more about community and creating an environment that's conducive to doing business. In that burgeoning desire to have a more holistic business, those other skill sets have become important. Especially if we want to be in business for a long period, relationships are the most important thing after we learn how to listen.

It was trial and error in the beginning when I was 21 or 22 and starting my business. I was young and excited, and I had a lot of energy that wasn't necessarily harnessed in any one direction. As I've matured, reflective listening has become a phenomenal practice for me. Learning about reflective listening in seminars or training has taught me to hear what people actually say instead of projecting what I need and want onto them. People appreciate that, and it gives me an opportunity to grow my business far more quickly than people who do not have that kind of listening skill.

So much is missed in conversations. I've learned the need to clarify that what I'm hearing is truly what they're saying and once I have that information, moving onto the next step is okay. So much is lost in dialogue because we all have so many different experiences and so many different needs and wants.

Having relationships and being able to listen, people will want me to succeed, and they help me to do so. I won't have to do as much heavy lifting because we're building something sustainable together, and not just because I need or want something, but because I care. The act of caring changes the way I do business in a way that people want to do business with me.

Whenever I came across people who were successful and had something that I wanted, I sought to understand why they were successful; how they were different from the other people who were just as good at what they were doing. I've never invented anything; I take other people's concepts and other people's work habits and repurpose them for myself. I'm creative with expanding on what other people are doing. It all comes down to listening and asking many questions, being curious, and then being creative with the information that I get. That's the only reason I am where I am today.

I'm at a point in my life where I love who I am, and there's such an expansiveness in that. There's so much that I want to share. My story is interesting and crosses over so many different paths, aside from the business path. There are just so many directions that I've gone that have brought me to this point, and I'm willing to share it.

I want to reiterate that I haven't done anything by myself. I don't work in a vacuum. I work with people, and every single resource is incredibly important. All of my successes are the result of the cumulative effort of everyone that I've ever touched, and everyone they've ever touched. I'm at a point in my life where I appreciate the challenges and believe that what I previously labeled as bad have definitely been the fruitful things to shape me as a person.

DAVID HALE

President and CEO, DHA, Inc.

www.dha-inc.com

Just because I find that I've made a mistake, I shouldn't stop my life; I shouldn't stop all that momentum I've built up. I have to keep going and adjust it as time gives me a chance.

I'm up early, and I'm in bed early. I'm prepared for the day before most people show up for work, and that can mean getting up at 4 o'clock, leaving the house at 4.40, and being at the desk by 5.30. For 25 years, it's been important for me to get in and be ready for what the day can bring. So many of us have experienced when their day was planned for this but went like that. Part of that is because we don't get our day moving before real life takes over.

As I moved into high school, I was a serious runner, and that required many morning runs before school. It forced me into the mindset of "Get up. Get the five miles in and get to school at the same time everybody else does". Four years of high school and then four years of college helped me to develop a pattern of behavior that can easily be maintained.

The other thing that I find to be the key to the day is to go to bed ready for tomorrow. That's something I don't hear many people talk about. My behavior the night before sets the course for the day ahead. If I go to bed with a whole bunch of extra items that I didn't get to, they're going to be piled on top of tomorrow's stuff. If I hit the sack prepared, when I wake up, I can hit the ground running.

I'm a list guy. I use Word to create lists. I have one for me, one for my home life, a list for my business, a list for my horse farm, a list for my race team and a list for each of my executives. On sheets of paper, I track them and take a pen, and throughout the day, I update where we are. I'm well up to speed as to where everything is.

I didn't have a great home life. I didn't have a great set of parents. I believe that everyone we meet teaches us either what not to do or what to do, and my parents taught me what not to do. That put a fire in me to be gone; to move on to my life; to get out from under that.

I was driven to excellence, as from my earliest beginnings I can remember wanting straight As, or graduating from high school with the highest grade point I could achieve, and getting into as many college options as I could. That was my driving force up until I got into college. Many people can relate to that feeling; it wasn't so much a drive towards something, as much as it was a drive away from something.

I had a couple of failures. I went to college convinced that I was going to be a geologist or a park ranger. During my freshman year in college, I realized I didn't enjoy the geology classes, and then I started researching what they made, and I said this wasn't going to support the lifestyle I desired. Luckily, freshman year is a bit of a generic year, so I didn't have to do much retooling. I chose computer science and I spent three and a half years doing that.

In the spring semester of my senior year, I could have graduated, but I didn't want to leave the cocoon of college yet. Life was never better than when I was in school. To remain a full-time student, I needed to take a couple of extra classes beyond what my major required, so I took Econ 101 as a spring semester senior, and I learned in that class that I picked the wrong major. I was drawn to numbers, to business, to finance and to leadership.

At that point, I had a job offer, so I took it. Rather than stopping my degree and restarting it, or dropping out of school with an identity crisis, I continued to move forward. I kept going and dealt with the emotion. When I realized I'd spent four years getting the wrong degree, I had a choice. I could freak out and give up, or slow down, or continue to build that momentum and push forward in life and make changes later.

I took the job, moved into it and as the years went by, I adjusted my career to leadership and business. It took me a few years to work through this. Little events cause us frustration. We get a little bit of frustration, and it builds until it turns into what I call my dragon heat. I'd feel that frustration and anger, and for years, I would burn people's heads off. I hurt people and damaged relationships, and caused trust issues.

Now I've become self-aware enough, through counseling, coaching and helping, to recognize when that process starts and head it off before it does damage. One of the things I've learned is not to look externally for an internal problem; not to look externally for a solution to a problem that's inside of me. That's what I've spent the last seven or eight years doing. I still read. I still listen. I still think about it. It's been quite a journey.

BARBARA BABCOCK

Vice-President and Treasurer, Woodward Landscape Supply

www.woodwardlandscapesupply.com

I tend to give people too many second chances. I want to believe people are going to come through, and that if they make a mistake or do something wrong, it's because they have some personal issues in the way and somehow or other they're going to get over that. While sometimes they do, many times, they don't.

I happen to be a morning person. So I've always been someone who was up early and did some of the most demanding work early in the day when I'm at my best. That was true whether I was studying as a student in school, or whether I worked in many of the jobs I've held, including this one. I tend to get much work done before most people's typical day starts.

I'm a time manager. When I was in my first career, I was fortunate to work in the computer industry for a large number of years. When I first started in that field, and as I went up the ranks, the companies that I worked for had a lot of onsite training programs for new managers. I got trained in such things as time management and that has taught me that it's so easy to get bogged down shuffling papers. One of the key things I remember about those classes was to try not to touch one piece of paper more than once. If I can deal with it and get rid of it, I deal with it and get rid of it. If it's going to take more time, I've got to prioritize. Anything I can get rid of quickly, I dispose of. So I try to get rid of all the noise quickly and then focus on the things that are more important.

For example, with administrative tasks — the things that are once and done, and can be done quickly — I try to get those done when it's okay to be interrupted. Then I can do something in three minutes, then another three minutes, and another three minutes. On the other hand, I do the payroll processing here. I can't be interrupted in the middle of that process, or I'll screw up paying people correctly. It's important to set those kinds of tasks aside for when I have some sustained focus time.

During the day, I could be working with a customer, I could be working with a vendor, I could be doing pricing, or I could be doing estimating. It's in and out, in and out, and in and out. I have a few free minutes here and there, so I try to do the tasks that are okay to do in a few minutes, as opposed to the ones that require more sustained concentration.

I've always been good with time. I've always done well in school. I have a quick mind. Probably one of my best gifts is that I'm good at generating alternatives whether that's to find a different product for a customer at a different price point or in a different color, or find a different supplier. All of those are alternative generating capabilities, and I'm good at it. I've always been that way as a puzzle solver.

It's part of the same thing. I've taken that love of solving problems and converted it into what I call generating alternatives as something I automatically think about when I'm presented with any challenging problem. I started doing that at a young age. I believe that's what got me through school with good grades and success. Moreover, it has made a difference as I've progressed through my professional career.

I tend to give people too many second chances, and that has cost me in keeping people onboard too long or giving them assignments that they didn't do well that hurt because they should have done a better job. I know I have that weakness, so I've become better at managing it, but it's still there. I've known this for some time, and I'm better at it.

I'm less likely to do it when there could be a real financial impact. I still do it, however, especially when there's going to be a people impact. For example, if I keep somebody on board too long that can't do the job, it impacts the people around them. It drags them down; it makes management have to work harder at getting things done. Although that's not a direct dollar impact, it has a financial impact.

It's not quite as terrible as when you let somebody, for example, drive a forklift and they always forget to put fluids in and burn up the engine and that costs you $10,000 to fix. That's a biggie. I don't make that kind of mistake anymore, although I'm sure if I think about it, that I could remember one or two times when I did in my younger years.

Many people don't understand that there is an opportunity cost involved in every choice we make in business, as well as in life in general. We have to consider not only the financial cost of a thing but also the cost regarding its energy and emotional drain. People are affected when somebody on the team is not pulling their weight.

Many of us have had the experience of working in a group and feeling like they're doing all the work, and yet somebody else is going to get all the credit. It certainly has a mental and emotional impact on members of the team when somebody isn't pulling their weight, aside from possible financial losses. Energy and mental focus are examples of things that we could lose by not being more diligent — and by giving too many second chances.

PART FIVE

MORNING ROUTINE

As expected, all of our supreme leaders have morning routines that are very well established. Their habits were surprisingly similar. We discovered that most leaders wake up early, exercise, and practice some form of thankfulness or mindfulness. Then they get to work.

While each leader had their routine, we collected a few that seemed to speak for the majority of most of the leaders we interviewed. It's clear that for these leaders, the early bird gets the worm!

FRED HABERMAN

Co-Founder and CEO, Modern Storytellers

modernstorytellers.com

My specific habits have played a massive role in my success, both personally and professionally.

I'm a night owl as I like the time alone. It's a time for me to think. It's also a time for me to read, or to watch television. It's a time for me to be. I've always gone to bed late, often around midnight. I start later, though, and as sleep is essential to me, I get an average of eight hours. I believe firmly that sleep and exercise are two crucial components of supreme habits.

I wake up and stretch. I do a little bit of yoga, maybe five to ten minutes to stretch my back and my body. I then make coffee, get the newspapers, and say hello to my dog and my cats. I try to get outside and look at the backyard for a little while and look at the flowers while the coffee's brewing. So immediately I have a happy experience with my animals and my backyard, and then I read the *New York Times* and the *Star Tribune*. Then if it's spring, summer or fall, three out of five days a week I ride my bike to work about nine miles. It's a great way to start the day because that time alone helps me to start thinking about the strategies of the day ahead. Interestingly, if I'm in my car, I often will start work quickly, so biking is a lot better. I can think about the more significant questions and challenges I'll face, and get my head and emotions straight because the work that we do is stressful. It's challenging stuff.

My specific habits have played a massive role in my success, both personally and professionally. There's no doubt about it. I need to create that personal space from sleeping to thinking to breathing to stepping away from the chaos to think as clearly as I can with all the challenges and problems.

When I don't do those things, I end up getting far more stressed out. I end up reacting far faster than I usually would, and can make the wrong decisions. There's no doubt that with exercise and eating better I feel better, and I'm able to be more flexible mentally. There's no doubt that when I go to bed, I have a similar routine.

When I go to bed, I always lie on my back and focus on my breathing for about 15 minutes, and then I fall asleep. I just let myself fall asleep, and a big part of that routine is meditation when I'm not in my thoughts and when I'm breathing through all the monkey thoughts, which helps clear the day as well.

Biking to work is a form of meditation for me as well. I can't emphasize the importance of meditation. It's the idea of being an outside observer and slowing down. It helps me not to get caught as quickly.

I had an independent nature early in life, and my parents still tell the story about how I wouldn't let my mom walk me to kindergarten as I wanted to do it on my own. I was involved in tennis and hockey and other sport. I have a side to me that's competitive and also a side that's very much a pleaser. The competitive side, the independent side, and the "I can do anything" mentality, combined with wanting to please everybody, weren't the healthiest things for me.

All through college, during the summers, I was the program director at Camp Manito-Wish, an Outward Bound type of camp, where I started leading canoe and backpacking trips, and I found that what I loved was this experiential learning and that the wilderness was my spirituality. It could slow me down, and allow me to look at a larger universe and see how we're insignificant yet powerful in the sense that we can feel.

So that's when I started to embrace this adventurous spirit that I have. I was the youngest program director in the history of the camp, which was stressful; however, I started talking to people about how it was the greatest job ever because we were doing what we were passionate about and doing it for people in a beautiful setting, and a supportive network and system. That idea of wanting to be around, and creating supportive communities, ideally in a wilderness setting, helped me create my basic mantra in life, which is to help people follow their passion. So that's what I've done.

BARRY SCHWARTZ

CEO, RustyBrick

www.rustybrick.com

I can't be an expert on everything. I focus on knowing something in the field that I'm in. I focus on becoming even smarter at that.

I'm an early bird. Usually, I start working around 5 a.m. when I wake up. I begin by responding to emails — sometimes numbering more than 70 — that I get overnight. In addition to the emails, I also go through a bunch of web feeds. I then send out some morning assignments and tasks and things that people should do.

I'm an Orthodox Jew, so I try to make morning services at the local synagogue, so that's usually around 6 a.m. Some people tell me they like to go for a morning jog or something like that. For me, it's more of a routine to go to the synagogue. It's the right thing for me to do. I try to get to the office between 6.30 and 7.

I'm into a routine of being consistent. Consistency is critical not just for my personal life, but also my business life. Letting the people around me know what to expect and when to expect it helps drive trust. It helps build that routine, which enables me to go through my work cycle in a way that's manageable.

People who are more up in the air and sporadic can never get through their list. Having that specific routine — that consistency of knowing between these hours I do X, Y and

Z — helps me manage my day and get through what I need to, and it helps our customers and our readers go through and understand what to expect from us and not be surprised by that.

When I get to the office around 9, I do a lot of writing. I write about search-engine optimization (SEO). I do that with two of the major SEO blogs on the Internet. I try to stick with that in the mornings.

After that, I focus on our core business, RustyBrick. I'll have filled out my calendar meetings and schedules with either clients or prospects. My calendar is usually quite full of conversations with existing clients, opportunities and internal meetings. Throughout the day, I'll speak to employees and handle the miscellaneous stuff, such as billing. At 1 or 2, I'll get the mail, and I'll handle all the billing related to that.

Every morning, before I get to work, I go through my bank statements and do that again every afternoon to make sure everything looks okay. I'm one of those who log onto the bank portal twice a day to make sure nothing weird happens there, just because it's a good routine to have. It allows me to handle any deposits or wires or credit-card deposits that aren't done through the manual deposits more efficiently. Some people wait to do it monthly, and then it becomes messy. I like to take care of things as soon as possible and not put things off until a later date. So I usually have that same routine throughout the day.

I rush to get many things done as fast as possible so that they get done more quickly than maybe they should have. Some people are more meticulous and take a longer time to do things, whereas I feel like speed is essential when I'm getting back to people. Maybe if I spend more time responding to emails or responding to specific requests, perhaps that would have led to better success.

It's a trade-off. People want fast answers in this world. It's like everything is immediate, so I try to respond as soon as possible, and I take zero me time. I do have a family, and it might take a toll on them and myself regarding health, but so far I've been able to handle that at least on some level.

CAROL COOK

Founder, The Music Room

the-music-room.net

I've a room in my house where I go to meditate. It's quiet, and I can shut the door. At that time of the morning, it's quiet outside as well. That's my plan to start my day.

I consider myself an early bird. In my younger days, I was a night owl, and maybe that shift happens to many of us as we get older. Over the years, I've come to find that my most productive times are in the morning. I'm a relatively early riser and get my day started early, usually between 4.30 and 5.

I'm not working that early typically, although sometimes that can be the case. I like to rise between 4.30 and 5 and do my exercising and my thoughtful meditation for the day. That seems to be helpful for me; when I started to adopt that behavior, the days became much more manageable.

I've dabbled in meditation for two or three years but started to get serious this year. I have a room where I go and sit in quiet. I do two kinds of meditation, I do a guided meditation that's visualization, and then I also try to get as still and quiet as I can and focus on breathing, and both of those things are quite helpful to me.

I became more serious about meditation because I'm getting married in October, and I have many irons in the fire with my business, so I wanted to make sure that I just enjoyed the process of my upcoming wedding. I didn't want to be stressed about it or anything else. I have a couple of advisors, one of whom is a spiritual advisor, who suggested to me that I start incorporating meditation into my day; that's what prompted it. I've been aware of it for a long time, I just hadn't been good at making it a daily thing, so that's what I've been doing this year.

The first thing was to make a conscious decision to meditate, and the second thing was to hold myself accountable by scheduling it. I try to make it the first thing I do, before I log on to any devices, or before the television comes on. When I start to realize that my mind is racing, especially if it's that early in the morning, that's a good indication and a reminder that I need to get in there and sit down.

I learned a long time ago to spin many plates at once, as I'm a serious multitasker. That's just something that I've been good at doing my whole life. I have the habit of planning my day, but also bringing in balance. If I don't get everything done that I had hoped to get done, I still go home. That's something that changed, as I used to stay until I got it done. I go back when it's time to go home, and I shut off everything.

Owning a business, I'm never shut off in my mind and my priorities. I try to get myself home and get into the next part of the day, whatever that might be. The business and everything that goes along with it will wait until the next day. The habit of balance has been one that took me quite a while to develop. In the early years of my business, I didn't have that, and I spent much time trying to do everything. In the last five years, I've improved and I've been able to detach a little bit. New business owners are emotionally attached to their businesses and with good reason. We're passionate about it, and that's why we go into business in the first place. Detaching is essential, however, because it allows us to restore and bring balance in so we can then start the next day again. That's been my goal and my practice.

I still struggle with trying to do everything myself. My biggest challenge has been and continues to be today, to learn how to delegate properly. I've improved at that, but my first instinct and reaction is to do it myself and what happens with that is that the people that are around you lose their power. I'm aware of it, and it's instinctive to me. That's probably the biggest thing that I struggle with, just because it's part of my nature.

CHRISTIAN SCHLEBACH

Founder, Hooley

hooleyusa.com

If I'm a self-starter, I'm making things happen. I'm not waiting for somebody to do it for me.

I'm an early riser. As I've become older, I've risen earlier and earlier. That's cool, because I get much done before everybody else is even awake. I usually wake up naturally about 5.30 every morning. That started about five or six years ago due to having two pugs. My dogs wake me up at 5.30, because they know that's what time I like to get up. Or vice versa. Things start happening around them because they sleep in our bed. I go downstairs, and I make a cup of coffee. My wife is still asleep. If it's the summer, I'll sit outside on our deck and have a coffee and catch up on the news and social media for about an hour.

I've got a good friend in town, and we do a lot of activities early in the morning. We'll go surfing or paddle-boarding in the harbor. Alternatively, I'll get a project done that needs to happen before it gets too hot. I've got several boats, so I'm always tinkering on those. There's always something to be done. So we'll paddle the harbor in the morning, or clean the boat. We also charter it, so I'll probably get ready for that. Then I'll come back and at about 7.30, my wife is just waking up, so I'll make breakfast, we'll eat together and then take the dogs for a walk in the graveyard next to our house. Then she goes off to work, and I go off to work, and that's our routine.

I always exercise in the morning. I make a point of getting my exercise in the morning because I'm too tired in the evening. I'm a natural exerciser. I eat well also, which is essential.

I'm a self-starter, so I'm always thinking down the line. I don't walk past something without taking care of it. I like to keep everything up that we own. With my business, I want to make sure everything's efficient and running smoothly, and all of our equipment is on point. I'm a jack-of-all-trades. I'm mechanical. I'm business-minded. I'm physical.

My habits have had a considerable role in my success. My habits drive my business, and my wife's driven too, and we've got a driven team here at our company, so it's a good little community, and we all help each other out and make things happen. We don't sit around. It's always busy, busy, busy. We can, however, also take time out and chill, which is a good thing.

I grew up on a beach in South Africa, and I had quite a loose childhood. My mom was mellow. I used to get up in the morning, get on a bus, go to school, get on a train and later come back, so we were quite self-sufficient. We always had to make our way home, either on a bus or hitchhike or whatever it was.

The beach was our playground. We'd be in the surf, we'd be window-bashing, we'd be jumping in the dunes, we'd be taking a walk down to the rec, which was about four or five miles down the beach. We were constantly outdoors.

I wasn't academic. I couldn't stand school. I loved sport. I didn't apply myself at school and I never went to college. I did reasonably well at the end of my exams because my mom threatened if I didn't do well that I had to pay back my private school tuition, and so I applied myself in the last three months. Then I got the call-up to the South African Navy. We all had to go as 18-year-olds after high school to either the army, the navy or the air force. I was called up to the navy, and the first three months of basic training was running around. I had to shave every day, even though I didn't need to shave, and I had to make my bed in the morning at 5 a.m. That experience molded me into being disciplined; into making my bed and getting up early.

My negative habit is that I invest much energy into people who aren't qualified enough. I get disappointed, and I assume they're just going to get it. That's probably my worst habit, and it's not a bad thing because sometimes it does work. I expect everyone to see what I see. My patience goes in there, and then I get disappointed. Sometimes I put a lot of eggs in one basket, and then end up losing the whole basket, and that can sometimes mean a relationship.

CHERI WILCZEK
Founder and President, ClinAudits, LLC
clinaudits.com

A leader of an organization is always bombarded.

I started ClinAudits after spending my career in the pharmaceutical industry. I felt like I'd hit a glass ceiling, so it was the opportunity after being downsized from a major pharma to start my own company. It was a big leap of faith, as I didn't know whether or not it was going to succeed. When anyone starts a company and has a family, that takes a great leap of faith since there's no certainty in terms of a paycheck.

ClinAudits is a global leader at supplying and performing clinical-research quality audits. Our focus is GXP, which encompasses good clinical practice, good manufacturing practice, good laboratory practice, good tissue practice and good pharmacovigilance practice within drug development and the industry. We audit anywhere from pre-clinical all the way through commercialization of a product.

I started the company in our home, and I made the big mistake of working in the company and not working on the company. I traveled every week for almost three years. My husband started to complain, so at Year 4, I had to start expanding to work on the company and not in the company. I hired more people and moved ClinAudits out of our home and into a *bona fide* office. Since that point, we've diversified into the clinical space, the manufacturing area and the laboratory area. It took a while.

We have more than 70 regionally-based auditors around the world. We have six people in our office that support those hardworking auditors who are always traveling. In the back office, we support not only our clients but our auditors. It's important to remember that these people in the office are focused on our clients, but they're also focused on our auditors. We have many masters, and we consider our auditors paramount. I believe employees are a company's biggest asset.

I'd always been a night owl until I married my husband. Since he's an early bird, I felt it was essential for us to be in the same time zone, so I became an early bird. Although I don't know what I'll be when I finally retire, there's some validity to being an early bird because it's quiet, you can think, and there's a certain peace in the world early in the morning that I like.

I do meditation in the morning. It's my time alone. There are times when I've had some of my best ideas in the shower when all I do is think. I think about the day. I think about some issues that might be coming up. I come up with good solutions in the shower. For me, that's my best time.

As the leader of an organization, I'm always bombarded. I've got sensory overload many days. It's imperative for leaders to take time alone whether or not it's just as I described early in the morning or on vacation. We have to have some time to think.

For me, we've always gone to the coast. The ocean is big for me in the sense of bringing peace and centeredness to me. I'm a big walker, so walking on the beach in the morning is an integral part of the day of the vacation because I can think. I can even start analyzing or developing different solutions for issues. That helps me.

One bad habit I deal with is procrastination. I've learned to reflect on that and discover the more profound answer. When I do procrastinate about something — and it doesn't often happen because moss doesn't grow at my feet often — if I have enough information to make a decision, I do it. I don't need to have 100 percent of the information, but I need to have enough to make me feel comfortable enough to move on it.

As I've become older, I think that when I find myself procrastinating, I have to discover the reason why I'm procrastinating. Is it that my gut is telling me something and I'm not tuned in? It's essential for procrastinators to be able to think through that because sometimes procrastination can be positive because it gives people a little bit of time to say, "Hey, why am I not moving on this?"

DAVE RYAN

Founder and President/CEO, High Resolutions

highresolutions.com

Everybody, I believe, is wired differently, and we each have a purpose.

Anytime anybody asks me to what I attribute my success, I can't at all shy away from the fact that I attribute my success to blessings from God. Because I'm a Christian, I feel there have been many things that have happened and transpired in my life that may not make sense. To an average person who's smart and educated, and has run businesses, many things that I do or that have happened to me may not make sense. They don't make sense to me either, and I think that I've been blessed and that success has been laid out in front of me, and opportunities have been given to me. I've been given favor through relationships that have been divinely orchestrated around me.

I look at being in business for 25 years as 25 years of growth rather than 25 years of habits. I do have patterns in my life that have proven to be successful, but I've certainly learned a lot over the past 25 years. No doubt I've changed the way I do things, and the way I approach things.

After 25 years, I'm still learning more habits and disciplines to build into my business. When you start employing more people who depend on you, everything changes. There's no secret formula. I've read many books lately about what other people do, and thought, "Hey, these are great ideas. I need to implement some of these as a growing business." I find myself continually praying and asking God for wisdom, opportunity and blessings.

I've worked hard and tried to take care of our customers, and hire the right people who are aligned with my mission and my way of thinking in the business. The people and the individuals I've surrounded myself with have been a significant influence on contributing to the success of the business.

When I say that I attribute my success to blessings from God, some of those blessings are related to specific skills or habits that I naturally have. There are certainly differences in people's personalities and skill sets, such as whether somebody's more of a right-brain or a left-brain thinker. Some people have more of an aptitude for risk, some people are more technical, some people are more artistic, some people are extroverts, and some people are introverts.

From a young age, I've had an entrepreneurial spirit, and it's hard-wired into me. Once, when I was a kid, my uncle lent me money to go to the store and buy flavored syrups to make snow cones. I pulled a red wagon around the apartment complex that we lived in selling snow cones. I had crushed ice in the cooler and little paper cups. I paid my uncle back for his loan. When I saw my profit, I realized, "Oh, this is how you make money!"

That led to many different jobs and many different little things that I've applied myself to where I could buy raw materials, and then be creative about turning it into something to sell, and figuring out how to make a profit on it. That went from snow cones to buying and selling goods, such as clothing and vinyl decals.

I followed a creative path, so I thought I would become a designer, and then through the opportunities that I never saw coming and never planned on, I led from the idea of being a designer and maybe working for an ad agency to getting more and more involved in graphics production. Then I became engaged in the operations of a startup business until I was running operations, and then the financials, and finally, I was running the business. My education on business financials never went past college Accounting 101.

This isn't the way I thought my life would turn out, but through relationships that God brought into my life, and the people who mentored me, or I had somehow gained favor with, everything happened. I got put into those different roles, and different seats until eventually, a few years ago, I was able to buy out my partner of more than 20 years.

I guess you could say that God smiled on me and continually blessed and guided my life, and that has yielded fruit and profits. For example, my partner gave me more and more responsibility, and it came to a situation in which he eventually looked at me as being his retirement plan. The baton of the business was handed over to me, and he completely exited the business.

LEE E. CORY
CEO, Paradigm Senior Living
www.psliving.com

We are constantly evolving, and this business is getting more and more challenging. I think adaptability, flexibility and patience are probably the three habits that have allowed me to build this business and continue to operate it for 25 years.

I've seen many people come and go, and many companies come and go. We take over distressed assets and fix them and solve them and try to figure out not only what happened and why, but how to ride the ship and get everything back to normal. Flexibility and adaptability are the keys in those actions. We also work to start new businesses and new communities, and that requires the same kind of discipline and energy.

At the beginning, when it's brand new, it's a happier time, and everybody is positive. When we're taking over a distressed asset, it's the opposite end of the spectrum, but it still requires the same skills. We have a limited amount of time and money to get both of those things done, whether it's a new one or a broken one and we have to stay incredibly focused and try not to get overextended with our commitments.

We operate in every time zone, including Alaska and Hawaii, so the phone rings constantly, and if it's a manager or a client, I'll answer 24 hours a day. I try to do most of the work in the morning and leave the evenings for peace and quiet unless somebody calls with an emergency.

I usually get up around 5, and I typically take about an hour to an hour and half a day just for myself, whether it's working out or meditation or doing something physical. With meditation, I've gone on and off with it over the years. Sometimes it's just sitting down and being quiet with my thoughts. I practiced transcendental meditation way back when it was the fad, and I remember the principles, but I'm not disciplined enough to do it twice a day every day.

I travel a lot, but the principles still apply even if we're not up to date with the practice. The physical part is more of a mental benefit than physical. I'm healthy and in good shape, but it wakes my brain up if I get up and run a few miles before I do anything else. Nine out of ten times, I tend to get that out of the way first thing.

One year, I had the goal to run every day for 400 days straight, and the qualifying run had to be at least three miles. There was no time limit, but if I didn't put in at least three miles, it didn't count. Then, however, I decided that I could destroy my knees if I kept that up, so I changed it and started doing other things. Now I still run a little bit.

While my habits have contributed to the success of my business, I've looked at other people who don't have the same habits, and some of them are incredibly successful. I wonder how long they can sustain that, and others were burned-out out altogether because they didn't take care of themselves. I have a goal to complete a 10k in my age group for the rest of my life. Right now, according to that theory, I'm ten years younger than I am, but it's a mental game. Running can be kind of boring, so I have to have some little game to play in my head to keep it interesting.

I started running when I was about 21. I ran a little bit in high school, and played basketball and ran track, but it wasn't a thing, it was just something I did because someone told me to. Running can become an obsession. I know people who have become obsessed with it, and it starts working against them at that point. So I try not to make it an obsession, but just a habit. It's something I know I need to do. If I miss a day, I'm fine. Some people if they miss a day, they're cranky and miserable and hard to be around, and it defeats the whole purpose of even doing those types of things.

Exercise has been a significant contributor to my success. I would encourage anyone who doesn't get up and move to do so because many folks that are in management and executive positions tend to spend much time on the phone or sitting down, or in meetings. We all have to get up and move.

Being in a senior business, our average customer is more than 80 years old. I talk to many of them about how I've been to sixteen 100th birthday parties in my life, and I've spoken to a lot of these folks at length about their lifestyles.

Good genes have a lot to do with it, but they tried to keep a positive outlook, and they got up and moved every day. Diet and all that goes along with it, but I've also known a few of them who had a horrible diet. They drank whiskey and smoked cigars, and they still made it to 100!

MARK JEWELL

Co-Founder and President of EPI-Q

www.epi-q.com

It's not an easy thing as a leader to put something I care about, like my company, into the hands of people who are so different from me. That requires a willingness to give up control that is difficult to find in leaders, yet is a mark of good leadership.

I've always been an early riser. I usually get up at 5 a.m. and work out, and then spend ten minutes in meditation. I use an app called Calm for a guided meditation. I use it mostly because it's not intrusive, and the music is the kind of peaceful music that facilitates that for me. I look forward to that each morning, and since my wife is an early riser too, if she sees I'm meditating, she will walk away. It's known that that's my time.

I've been meditating off and on since my thirties, and I'm 60 now. In the last five or six years, it's become a routine practice of mine. I wouldn't say that it was occasioned by anything in particular, but I became aware that there was so much noise in life. I get into the office setting, and things can go crazy.

Meditation has helped in focusing my energy and ability to stay calm in the face of conflict and often competing demands. One was the business. The second was health. I also felt that after working out, I needed time to cool down, and that evolved into the meditation practice as part of that cool-down period. So I've used it as a health-related benefit as well. I had some issues with marginally high blood pressure, and thus exercise and the meditation combined got that under control.

Our business is in the healthcare field, so I'm attuned to the fact that people look for pharmaceuticals as an easy out. Additionally, I've always struggled with weight, and I have to work out and be conscious of my diet. My weight has fluctuated over the years as has my ability to cope with things. I keep up a constant strength and rely on self-control and discipline, and social support to help manage the things I feel I can't control.

I'm not a Type A person, so I'm not driven by an innate tendency towards one type of behavior. Playing sport and being part of a team helped me as I was an avid baseball and football player. I'm certainly not built for that long-term, but during the growing-up period, that was something I enjoyed. To compete at a higher level, I found that there are things I have to build into my routines, such as practice, self-control, discipline and social support.

My habits have shaped the kind of style and culture that we've created here at the company. For example, I get distracted easily, and I'm terrible with details. As a result, I've learned along the way that the best way to be successful is to hire people who are different from me. I employ people who are smarter than me, and people who have attention to detail, and then I give them the autonomy to make mistakes and do what they need to do. Being aware of habits can either be helpful — if we understand them and can address them head-on — or they can ruin us.

Hiring people who are smarter or different from me, or maybe even more talented in other areas — especially areas where I lack — and then giving them autonomy to make mistakes, takes a level of maturity and trust in the process. In order for that to be successful, I have to create ways for them to feel like it's theirs as well, so they may not own a piece of the company, but if I tie incentives and reward them for being successful, they have a vested interest in making sure that my interests align with their interests.

MIKE HAMEL

Owner, HMA Contracting
www.hmacontracting.com

The first thing I do when I get up in the morning is practice gratefulness.

When I was younger, I didn't have the best discipline. My parents did bring me up with a hard work ethic, but I didn't get to the point where I was disciplined until my twenties. That was when I realized I'd better get my stuff together and started working hard. In my late twenties, I got involved with a lot of self-development, and that's kept everything going for me ever since. When I found self-development, it cranked me right up, and I don't ever want to stop.

I do many things that Tony Robbins teaches and practices. I refined a lot of things about myself around goal setting and how I control myself and keep my days going the way I want them to go. There have been many people who advise, but Tony Robbins has always been my choice over the years to help me out.

My habits have had everything to do with my success. I wasn't disciplined early on, but I'm very disciplined now. I get up at the same time every morning. I do the same morning rituals — my workout, my affirmations, my mindfulness. I've been doing that for years. It's all my psychology more than my mechanics at this point. Moreover, I've been practicing them easily since my early thirties.

The first thing I do when I get up in the morning is practice gratefulness. It's not about religion, but it's just a connection with God. In other people's minds, it may be the universe, but it's God for me. I start my day by thanking him for everything I have in my life, and I run down all of the things that I'm grateful for.

That's always my family, my businesses, my relationships and my health. I've been doing that for years. Then I get up and work out; I run or I lift weights. My working day probably doesn't start for two hours after I get up. I have two hours to myself, and that's kept me going for years and years.

My experience started in probably my early thirties when I began practicing some morning rituals, incantations, affirmations, running and walking. When I found it, I didn't want to give it up. Because when I got into working out, I was that person. I've always been an early riser, so I would get up, grab the coffee, eat a little cereal, get in the car, and start right to work. That's a different feeling. We all have stress, but it's a whole different feeling. In my early twenties, if I wasn't eating, I was bored. Moreover, I felt more stressful in my twenties than I do now in my fifties.

It's about training myself and my brain, and it's just amazing how things fall off for me, and I won't absorb the negative as often. It just doesn't affect me, even some of the bigger things. Because of the mindfulness and where I am constantly, it becomes a different mindset.

Mindfulness takes practice. It helps if I practice self-development. Some days, I'll be reading some great things. Other days, I'll be listening to great tapes. Other days, I'll be listening to unbelievably empowering music. It's every day. Those are the habits I've developed, and they didn't happen overnight. That's what people have to realize. I discovered it and never stopped because it makes me feel phenomenal.

Not only does it not happen overnight, but it doesn't happen by default. It's not the default position to do the thing that's uncomfortable. It's so much easier for us to wake up, open our phones, and scroll through Facebook, Twitter, Instagram or LinkedIn. We can blow a bunch of time first thing in the morning and then do the same thing at night.

That's not taxing on my mind. It's not taxing on my spirit. It feels less difficult in the short run. In the long term, however, I'm not improving myself, and I'm not growing. I have to work hard to get over that default of just doing what's comfortable.

That's also where the exercise comes in, which is specifically cardio for me. I try to mix it up, but I do some running. I do some biking. I do some lifting. I rarely set the alarm, and I would say the alarm goes off 10 percent of the time. This morning at 3.45 I woke up and was at it. I did my mindfulness as that's been a habit of mine for a long time.

I love the early mornings. At 4.45, the birds start chirping. I can always count on the birds. In the Northeast, they chirp around 4.45 every morning, so I can hear them, and it's great. When I go out for my run at 5, they're right out there with me. It's amazing. I'm 53 now, and I've just been living this stuff for a few decades, and I love it. I always make time for it.

DAVID MUNN

President and CEO, ITSMA

www.itsma.com

Exercise is something that's important to me, even when I travel, to stay in shape and stay healthy. It's something I greatly enjoy doing.

I work out and exercise many times a week. There are certain mornings when I go for a run or a bike ride or a swim, and I'll get up earlier in the morning to do that first. Other days, I get up, have a cup of coffee, look at emails to see what I need to respond to, eat, plan out my day, and review my activities.

We're all creatures of habit. What I eat, what I do, what I like to do, those things have helped give me energy, and time for creativity to think and plan. In any business that's moving fast, we can get into a grind that can eat us up. So exercising, eating well and other things that I do help me feel like I can stay ahead of what I need to accomplish and want to achieve in any given day or any given week or month.

If I had to choose one particular habit that I might attribute to my success, it would be around sleep. Some people say they don't need much sleep, whereas I need at least six hours. When I get seven hours of sleep, well that's even better. I manage that activity. Exercise is a huge part of what I do. I eat three or four meals a day as I need fuel to think and act and exercise and do those things. Those are regular habits. I rarely go a day without orange juice, a banana, cereal and a cup of coffee in the morning.

There are some things that growing up in the household in which I grew up have influenced who I am today. I learned the work ethic, hard work, getting up and getting after the day. Continual and continuous learning and goal setting has been key. Having strong friendships, relationships and networks has always been important to me as well. While growing up, these things were a big part of my life and continue to be a big part today.

I played sport all year round, and I was very active. I did go to bed earlier and was up early to start working on and developing things. The hard work and resourcefulness are things that you learn early. I had the biggest paper route in our town. Part of it was the goal to be able to handle that many accounts, to be able to collect that much money, and also have money that I could use towards investing in things I wanted. It sounds funny, but a better bike, and having the ability to get more things for me weren't part of the regular family budget. I had to take action.

As a business leader, I have to have vision, be creative and a great communicator, hire and mentor and coach people. In the business we've run, we have many people who have been here for a long time. Most have developed well and are incredibly productive. The habit of being more selective, whether it's about certain friends or employees is critical.

I have to know when to cut ties and be open to communication, which can sometimes be difficult messaging. Even to this day, there are mistakes I've made in hiring, coaching, and mentoring certain people. That's something I continue to look at. What do I need to do to get better at selecting people to join the company? How could I have mentored or coached someone better to get the most out of them? How can I know the right time to part ways?

From a role standpoint, before I joined and helped build ITSMA, I started in market research as an analyst. After three years, I went to business school to study strategy, marketing and business leadership. I then spent time with Oracle and Apple in sales and marketing roles. All of those experiences have helped me be successful at ITSMA.

We work with a wide range of leading technology, telecom and professional service organizations to advance their marketing processes. We have a great team of researchers, trainers, consultants, sales, business operations, customer success, customer experience and finance individuals. We operate in multiple countries and work with organizations all over the world. So it's been a great ride so far, and now we're celebrating our 25th year in business.

ZEL BIANCO

Founder, President and CEO, Interactive Edge

www.interactiveedge.com

It comes down to three things, and one of them is the fact that I go to the gym every single day.

Sometimes I run outside, sometimes I run at the gym. If I miss a day due to travel, I feel bad about it, because it's become such a habit; not only for health purposes and keeping me in shape and looking young and feeling young, but it also clears my mind. It also allows me, even if I've had a stressful morning, to come back to the office feeling revitalized and a little less stressed so I can deal with whatever comes my way that afternoon. The members of staff appreciate it when I get to the gym as regularly as I do, because it makes for a much more productive way of dealing with stress. It has become a habit, and I feel it when I don't do it.

I'll give my wife credit because she is a big runner. She's run four New York City marathons, and my daughter as well. My wife and my daughter, Elizabeth, have four New York City marathons under their belt, and a whole bunch of Brooklyn half marathons. They convinced me to go out with them. They ran the Big Sur marathon out in California. I ran the half marathon. I always ask them, "What is it that makes you want to do that?" It's just a sense of accomplishment, and that's the same reason I go to the gym every day.

Another habit is looking at the idea of taking risks and never giving up. A side or a branch off from that is that from an early age, I developed a way for people to trust me. My parents came from Italy, and they did not have much money. I come from a family of two brothers and two sisters, so it was always expected that we would work.

Whether it was a paper route at an early age or pumping gas at a gas station on a Sunday or caddying at the local country club, it all had to do with developing a work ethic. As a teenager, the owners of the gas station trusted me enough to be by myself all day on Sunday so that they could be with their families. They would come and check in, maybe towards the afternoon to make sure everything was okay, but my ability to exude trust and confidence played into it when I started this business with my wife 25 years ago.

We had two small children at the time, so we took a considerable risk of starting this little interactive multimedia company from the spare room at our condo in Connecticut. I remember my wife's dad saying to me, "Oh my God! Zel is a dreamer. He's got these big dreams."

That, however, is when I had to believe in myself, and I had to be confident in myself. My first client, which happened to be Johnson & Johnson, had to trust me enough to take a chance on a tiny little company with no track record whatsoever. When we had been introduced to this client by someone that I knew, we had still been in the spare bedroom in the condo, and this gentleman from Johnson & Johnson said, "Well, I always make it a point to visit a new vendor, so before I can give you business, I want to visit your place of business." We had to scramble. We, therefore, put him off for about a week to get it done, but we had to come into Manhattan, find an office space that was at least presentable, and get it set up so that we actually had a physical office instead of working out of our home. That was where it started. Getting that first piece of business from Johnson & Johnson allowed us to then to get that second piece of business, which was Nabisco.

My point is that we had to take a significant risk, and then we had to be confident in being able to deliver those services over the software that we were selling at the time to get that second and third client. It was a lot easier when we had got one or two or three under our belt. It's much more difficult when there's no capacity to name drop.

Interactive Edge was chosen as one of the ten most recommended retail-solution providers in 2018. So we certainly have some success to show aside from keeping things going for the past 25 years.

JACK EBERT

Founder, South Atlantic Insurance

www.satlanticins.com

I can't change my height or maybe the way I look, but I can change my habits.

I founded the insurance agency 25 years ago, and we specialize in truck insurance, which is a niche market specifically for large trucks, such as the 18-wheelers. I didn't have much of a sales background before I started the company, but when I started selling, I came to enjoy it. By the way, the sales that we do happen 99 percent over the phone.

I started as a commercial limo driver and drove a stretch limo taking people to the airport, weddings and other occasions. I was asked by a couple to be their chauffeur, and they happened to be in the insurance industry. I drove for them for about three months, and when they saw I had a knack with people and liked my personality, they got me involved in their business.

Helping them grow their business gave me the skills I needed to start my own business. I worked for them for approximately five years. The last two years I was with them, they had a truck insurance agency that I helped run for them, and then I opened up my own. Being a limo driver and becoming an insurance agent is similar to the person who sweeps the stage on Broadway and then becomes the lead actor in the show.

I'm an early bird now, but I wasn't always, just for the last 20 or 25 years. When I get up in the morning, I like to spend the first 30 minutes of my morning praying and reading the Bible. I also like to work out in the morning at the gym or to go for a bike ride. My morning habits serve two purposes. One, it gets my spirit going by praying and reading the Bible. Two, it gets my physical body going by having a workout.

Having those two different habits I've acquired over the last 25 years has kept me on a specific schedule. I don't have to think about what I'm going to be doing. As a planner, I plan things, and I make notes on my iPhone. So on top of my morning ritual, I have my plan for the day. I need to be organized because if things change and I don't have a plan, I could be all over the place.

I focus my efforts on how I have to do these things. So if I have ten things I have to do, I know the five that must be done first, and I prioritize them, and I'm fairly disciplined with that. I was in martial arts from the age of 20 to 36, and I developed a great discipline. It's almost like being in the military when doing martial arts. I was able to get black belts in a couple of different styles of karate, and that helped with my discipline.

I used to struggle with procrastination in getting things completed. I'm not perfect, but I have changed that by 80 to 90 percent from where I used to be. I used to procrastinate all the time, and someone can label themselves as a procrastinator but that can be changed. Someone can label themselves as always angry; that too can be changed. Everything can be improved. So while procrastination was once a negative for me, now that I've been able to overcome it, I'm more successful.

People can miss out on particular areas of their lives where maybe they're all about business and they don't take care of their health. In their late fifties, they can have what they call the widow-maker and die, and then they can't enjoy the fruits of their labor. We have to savor the moments and enjoy the journey along the way of life. We can't just say that when we're older or when we retire, we'll enjoy life. We need to enjoy today, not to be reckless of course, but to enjoy today. If we take care of our health now, and take care of our spiritual well-being now, in the later parts of life, we'll be successful and be able to enjoy those years. If we can't enjoy it, then why would we do all that work?

I used to work sometimes 15 or 16 hours a day, six or seven days a week for ten years. That was way out of balance, but it was something I needed to do in my business. Now I'm working 20 hours a week. Now I'm able to enjoy life. I'm sitting in my North Carolina home in the mountains at this time. I also have a home in Florida that we go back and forth to enjoy.

We should work hard in the beginning, or else we won't be able to enjoy it later. We may want to think about what's going to happen tomorrow, but we have to plan and keep ourselves in a position where we'll be productive.

PART SIX

READING AND WRITING

Leaders read, and leaders write. Naturally, anyone in a position of leadership is going to be on a path of learning. Most leaders tend to have bookshelves or Kindles packed with books that teach them how to refine their craft, their industry, their business and their ways of being.

We were curious to learn what books these CEOs, presidents and founders read. As expected, we discovered that they read the leadership classics. We found that they also read books in other areas to inspire their way of leading.

Additionally, many executives feel the need to write books of their own. They're driven to make their mark on the world of leadership and to contribute their learning, strengths and thoughts to the marketplace.

ALAN CROWETZ

CEO, InfoStream, Inc.

www.infostream.cc

As an owner of a technology company, you'd never guess that I read science fiction.

Strangely enough, I always wanted to go into the corporate world. I had this vision around 25 years ago of being a vice president or president of a Fortune 500 company, such as IBM or Microsoft. No matter what I did, I kept getting redirected towards technology. People would find out that I had computer skills.

Even if I was working in the accounting department or the marketing department, before I knew it, I was redirected over to the I.T. department. I always wanted technology to be a turbo boost to my career, but not my primary function. After that had happened enough times, I developed a few clients on the side and would help them out here and there for some extra money.

After the second or third time of being redirected, I jumped ship and started working full-time in technology. It was a significant shift for me to stop thinking about running a Fortune 500 company and be entrepreneurial instead. I started helping small and medium-sized businesses by providing I.T. support to numerous different kinds of firms in South Florida.

I jokingly say I'd rather stay up all night long if I had to be up early the next morning than go to sleep and have to wake up early. I'm a night person. I'm focused on getting to work on time. Then, once I get to work, my primary morning routine is to clear my desk. I want to get all the different loose ends out of the way so I can focus on more strategic and bigger picture things. That usually means getting all the emails caught up, phone calls done, cleaning, clearing off the desk of any loose ends and being ready to get focused on whatever is on my plate for the day.

My chief blessing and maybe my curse is my type A personality. I'm focused on getting things done. I'm the guy who enters a project due in three months, and I don't wait until the end; I want it done in the first three days so that I have three months to goof off. That's probably the most significant factor that has led to my success.

Ironically, in recent years, it has caused me a few hiccups, and I've had to learn to adjust it. I've always been focused on the next goal, the next hurdle, where I need to be, whether it's planning, or tactically getting through a problem. Being proactive is a habit.

I'm focused on beating deadlines and staying on track. I always have a to-do list, and I live off my to-do list and constantly re-prioritize my tasks. Sticking to that method is one of the habits that is a big part of what I do.

Even though I have electronic means for creating to-do lists, I have a legal pad next to me that I'm always keeping track of and using to make sure that I'm on target. It's so easy these days to get distracted or to go off mission, so my focus is to make sure that I'm always working on what's essential and not chasing every shiny object that comes across my radar. I live on those freaking things. I tear through them, and everybody yells at me to use technology. Even though I own a technology company, I can't make the switch.

I've been reading since childhood, and I'm an avid reader. I know the big thing these days is to read the business books, and there's value in those. For me, it's not so much books on motivational leadership; although I do read those, the vast majority of what I read is not in that category.

For the business side, I'm a big fan of articles. There are a lot of consolidated services, such as Flipboard, where you can find many articles on particular areas of interest. I also like to read articles, blogs and biographies on successful people. If Richard Branson has something that he feels is important to tell people, I want to be listening to that, for example.

One of my favorite business books is *The E-Myth*. As far as tactical business things are concerned, this quarter, I'm interested in marketing and trying to find ways of thinking outside the box from my competition. I'll be tearing through tons of articles to find tips, and I have Google alerts set up for specific keywords. Next quarter, I'll flip that to another area of focus that I want to develop.

I read quite a wide variety of things, including history. I like quantum physics as I find it fascinating and somehow I've become deeply interested in that over the last decade. My go-to for relaxation is science fiction. I also read a lot of social media and news.

I've thought about writing a book a million times. The weird thing is I'm 50/50 between writing a business type book, as I have a few ideas on that one, or writing something entertaining. I've been close a few times, and have made outlines; I enjoy writing so I suspect I could whip out something fairly quickly and easily.

It does sound intriguing to have someone write a book for me. I have to pick and choose where my most limited resource is going to be spent. The older I get the more I realize it's my time that's my most valuable thing and it has to be worth it for me to invest my time in anything.

DARIUS SAMANI

Founder and CEO, VersaSuite

versasuite.com

I read a great deal about history because I don't believe the human brain has changed much in the last 40 or 50 thousand years. We are still the same selfish bastards that we were 50 thousand years ago.

Mornings are quiet. I can think. I am fresh. I can do better, I think better, and I make better decisions. I make most of my decisions while I'm driving to work early in the morning because there is no traffic, and I take that time to contemplate and plan for the day.

I usually get up and check my emails, if there are any urgent emails to tackle. Otherwise, I take a shower and come to work and do most of my primary work commitments for the day. I look at my calendar the night before, as well as early in the morning on the day. My fairly hectic day starts at about 9 o'clock when I have my first meeting, and after that, I try to have no other meetings until late in the afternoon so I can get some work done.

The early morning meetings are the most beneficial as they give me a review of what has happened the day before and what needs to be planned for the day. I have meetings with separate groups, no more than ten minutes each, and sometimes only five minutes. We review the major tasks to tackle for the day and those that we were supposed to be working on the day before.

I usually get to work between 5 and 6 a.m., and I typically don't leave until about 6 p.m. When I get home, I spend about an hour or thereabouts either doing some exercise or doing some yard work to get my mind off work and relax. I'll have a light dinner and then spend two or three hours reading or checking email. Now and then, I watch a movie, and I generally go to bed at about 10.

I am a history and philosophy major, and history is my passion. I read many books about history. Understanding how people behaved two hundred or two thousand years ago, and how they acted in the recent past, gives me quite a bit of indication about human nature. It helps me lead effectively. Each time I return to books I read years ago, I learn something new. I know how profoundly historical characters or personalities of major historical figures have impacted the historical path and the directions. I try always to have one or two books to read at a time. Recent books that I have been reading include a book on Franklin D. Roosevelt, which I liked a great deal, and there's a historical book called *Paris 1919*. It's about how the foundation was set post-war for the division of Europe and the Middle East. I've found it astonishing and interesting.

The specific time periods I enjoy learning about include the recent past. I have followed since 1980 all the historical events and all the major historical events that have taken place. I've not only just followed them, but have tried to understand how they happened. What brought the collapse of the Soviet Union? If you understand those parameters, a lot of it is business related, and we can apply the same parameters to business. The beauty of it is, those events are now well documented, and the personalities have played profound roles. For example, Gorbachev tried to rescue the regime, but it was too rotten from within, and it collapsed. Those realizations are profound and we can learn a great deal from studying history.

ERIC MILLER

Co-Owner, Padt, Inc.
www.padtinc.com

I always take the time to learn a new skill or learn something I don't know, and that's a strong habit for me that I enjoy, but it also helps me from a business perspective because I know about all these different things and I can do a lot with this knowledge.

A lot of our success has to do with the people around me, such as having great employees and two great partners. We all complement each other. As for my shortcomings, having people around me who don't have the same shortcomings is good. My positives complement their shortcomings. What's made it work is focus and determination. The process may not be disciplined, but we get it done, and we get it done efficiently.

One of my strengths is that I've always been a reader. I devoured the whole Hardy Boys set, and because my mom loved Agatha Christie, I read all of her Agatha Christie books when I was quite young. Then I started devouring science fiction in sixth and seventh grade. I've been a big reader since then. I love to read, although I listen to books more now because I can do that while I'm doing other things, I go through two to three books per month.

Almost everything I read will influence me to some extent. The early writings of Isaac Asimov, especially a book called *Caves of Steel*, had an impact on me when I was young. It's about robots and the way future society might live. He got some of the technology wrong, but a lot of it he got right, and that was an influential book for me. Probably, the other book that had significant influence on me from a nonfiction standpoint was a biography of John Adams. I'm a multifaceted person, but I think John Adams is the kind of person I'd like to be. He was practical. He was well-educated. He looked at things on an individual basis rather than from a party or a personal standpoint. He didn't succeed as well as he probably should have, but much of what this country is today is due to his thoughts and way of looking at the world. When I read his biography, it resonated with me strongly. I was somewhat into my career at that point, so it had a substantial impact on me. A lot of the structure of the government was his idea. He was the one who came up with the push to break away. He may not have been the one who spoke up about it, but he got the more vocal folks like Jefferson and Franklin and Washington to do the work. He contributed to a lot of the thought behind it.

Especially in reading the letters that were in the addendum to the book, it was interesting to see how he looked at the world, particularly in his letters to his wife. Philosophically, that whole enlightenment was done right. The French Revolution didn't go well, whereas the American Revolution did quite well, and I'm fascinated by the reasons why it did so. They believed in a balance of power and moderation and not giving too much. Even if someone feels that he's the right person who's doing good for the people, he shouldn't have that kind of power.

When we don't set a far goal, of course, we don't make it, and when we go all out, the ends can justify the means. This is what I love about that period. Most especially, I like to consider the level of pressure it would've taken for a person to turn from loyalist to rebel or patriot. The choice had to come into people's homes before they cared.

People didn't want to choose a side a lot of the time until they had British soldiers quartered with them, and then it became real. It's valuable to look at the inaction of so many people, even today. Maybe it's because it hasn't come to their front door yet.

I wrote a book called *Better Blogging for Your Business*. I self-published it, and I've sold a few copies because I haven't promoted it, so it's not going to go anywhere, but I did write a book. I've been running the company blog for quite a bit of time and had written a couple of articles about blogging for business. It was one of those things where I've never written a book. I decided I was just going to write a book, so I did. I sat down and wrote it. It hasn't been professionally edited or anything, but it's out there, and I sell a copy every once in a while.

GUY TOLEY

Co-Owner, Claire Pettibone

clairepettibone.com

I'm a lifelong learner, but I have not always been a reader.

Claire's my wife, and we started our fashion apparel business in 1994, the same year we got married. Claire is a designer, and I manage the operations and handle the general director duties. Our primary focus at this point is couture bridal.

I tend to be a burn-the-candle-at-both-ends person. I could start my day early and go late, depending on what's required at a given time. I'm generally an early bird though. That's when I like to wake up and sit in a quiet space and use that time to reflect and think about the day ahead and get some ideas regarding planning and things like that.

I'm a lifelong learner, but I have not always been a reader. That's one of the things that I've had to pull into my life and adopt. Going back to when I started in school, I didn't go to kindergarten or preschool or anything. I started first off at first grade. From there, I was behind on a lot of things. From there, reading wasn't something that was at the forefront for me.

Going back, maybe 10 or 20 years ago, I realized I needed to make an effort on reading. I don't read a lot for pleasure. I don't read a lot of novels or that sort of book. I have read some, and I do like them, but I tend to go for books that have much weight to them. For example, I just downloaded the complete works of Aristotle. Not that I seek to be a grand philosopher, but those are the sorts of things I read. For me, it's like I'll take the first book and read a few pages, digest it, sit with it, let it go for a few days and then pick it up and get back to it again. That's the way I get through books like Aristotle's at this particular point. I also enjoy other books that tend to help me with my quest to learn why we are here. What is all of this about? I like to read about things we all start wondering about at a certain age.

The one book that influenced me in connection to the work that we do and I thought was interesting was *The Pillars of the Earth* by Ken Follett. It's a thick book that spans a lifetime of the building of a cathedral in the 12th century. It follows a family, and how they connect, and the noblemen and the sheriff and the tax collector. There is political intrigue, and many interesting stories regarding the way religion met politics. What influenced me was learning about the masons and the other people who do the work. When I started reading the description of why people did the job they did and why they fell in love with the work they did, I began to think about that concerning my work and then also the work of the people who sew our garments. We produce everything here, and have always made that a part of our business model, the craftsmanship and what people do. There's a pride in the work that people do.

When I started reading that book, I started thinking about that regarding the people that work for us from all levels and top to bottom and how it's all connected. No job's more important than any other job. It all has to make sense, and it all has to be there, and everybody who is touching a garment and putting something into it is placing a piece of their spirit in it, and that has to be respected, and we do so.

ANNETTE HAMILTON
CEO, Ho-Chunk, Inc.
hochunkinc.com

I've always been a diligent reader, and that has been a habit that I've carried forth in my life. I've been a reader of a lot of different genres and a lot of different opinions.

I'm the chief operating officer for Ho-Chunk, and we are the economic development corporation for the Winnebago Tribe of Nebraska. What we do for a federally recognized tribe in rural Nebraska is help them through developing a business infrastructure, creating jobs on the reservation through a business, and building an economy. Because we're used to working at a business pace, we take the sum of our business experience and help develop the reservation.

We have a unique model where I get to operate as a for-profit, and that's our first and foremost directive, but we also get to reinvest that money in developing the reservation in a rural part of Nebraska that hasn't historically had much development. We've expanded into home ownership, and created a whole Ho-Chunk community development corporation that focuses on housing and a Ho-Chunk village that provides housing and places for business entrepreneur shops and has brought in a Dollar General.

I get to be the coordinator of the operations on the internal side of things. I feel very fortunate to have the job I do. We deal with systemic poverty on the reservations. The rural parts of this reservation in Nebraska, have not had the opportunities that other places have had. It hasn't had home ownership. It hasn't had lots of different things. We try to take the profits that we make and reinvest them to make a big difference.

Just this year, we commissioned an economic impact study. We have been able to increase jobs for tribal members who have a bachelor's degree by close to 65 percent. We've increased jobs not just on the reservation but in the entire surrounding area. We're in the northeast portion of Nebraska, so we're close to Iowa and South Dakota. We're having a tremendous impact. We've created home ownership where there hasn't been home ownership before. It does make my heart get a little bit bigger.

When I was a kid, I read a comic strip with Cinderella and her fairy godmother. The fairy godmother had her sparkly magic wand, and Cinderella was waving her arm away and the caption read, "Forget the prince, I want an M.B.A. from Stanford!" I cut that caption out and put it on my corkboard as that was when every child had a corkboard instead of a computer. That corkboard followed me around until I was an undergraduate.

We lived in poverty when I was young. We grew and canned our vegetables, and raised chickens both to sell and eat. There was no money for clothes or coats or anything. I was so focused on survival, and that caption meant everything to me because at that time I didn't know what an M.B.A. was. I didn't truly understand the prestige of Stanford yet either, but what it meant to me was that there was a way out of poverty. It was a way to fulfill some kind of purpose that deep inside as a young kid I just knew I had. I was so convinced of that that I drove my mom crazy all the time saying, "Come on, we have work to do. Tell me what my purpose is! Let's get moving on it."

I didn't have many role models as there weren't a lot of women executives in business, at least none that I knew. I knew I wanted to do something with business. Even when I was raising chickens, I joined the Future Farmers of America, and tracked the profit and loss. I tracked whether selling the eggs was enough to justify raising the chickens; or how much we supplemented by eating them versus having to buy them. I always had a business mindset.

I've always been a reader. At a young age, my mom would find books and different things for me to read. When I was a kid, there wasn't a phone where you could look things up. Even though we were poor, my mom found a way to get an encyclopedia set, so I was regularly reading from that and other books. She also took us to the library to give us access to anything we wanted to learn. Back in my day, the library was the Internet.

I read any of the genres. I was a big Nancy Drew and Hardy Boys fan as a kid. That taught me how to figure out positive solutions or how to figure out puzzles and try to unlock something. That turned to historical fiction, to self-help books, and now to a combination of business education and some light, humorous reading.

One of the books that made an impact on me — and not necessarily in business — was when at a young age my mom assigned a whole range of different books for me to read. One of the books was a shorter book by Ayn Rand, but then I quickly went to her novel, *Atlas Shrugged*. That's a heavy-duty book to read when in junior high or high school. I probably didn't understand all of the different philosophies and messages that she was trying to get through. What it said to me, however, was that I could make a difference in my life and that there was a possibility that I had control of my destiny. I think back on that book quite a bit, as it changed my life.

I also enjoyed *Expect to Win* by Carla A. Harris. It addresses questions such as how to promote ourselves; how to expect to win; how to set the stage; how to do it and still be authentic to ourselves; and how not to share too much while still being our authentic selves. We don't have to take out other people. We can build up people and build ourselves up too. I've heard her speak at a couple of events and I've taken a lot from that book.

She shows how to keep our integrity and authenticity. We can still be ourselves. So whatever our strengths are, we can play them up and use them. When we're more genuine, people are much more attracted to that, as it's just much more believable.

As a woman in leadership, I can get a little too much into my head. At least myself, I don't want to speak for anyone else. Sometimes we have to be something that we are not, and this was a real-world example of how she used her strengths and her qualities to be an authentic leader, and to gain trust and how she built herself up without tearing other people down.

MICHELLE MANIRE

President and CEO, Coast to Coast Conferences & Events

ctcconferences.com

Now that I have so much expertise, I want to share it.

I love reading. One of my favorite books is *Go-Giver*. It's a perspective on life and a perspective on business that first we want to see how we can give to others and open ourselves up to receiving. It works. For example, do we believe what we're offering is going to benefit the person that we're reaching out to? It's a different mindset than being tenacious about closing deals. It's instead asking what we can give to the other person.

I like the type of book that puts things in perspective. I read a lot of different business books about different cultures. Culture in business is huge right now. As the unemployment rate goes down, we know better what our culture is and can be working on it at all times. I belong to a mastermind and also to the Women's Business Enterprise Council. We're continually talking about business and how things are changing rapidly. We've got to keep up with the changes.

I teach my staff that our purpose is to provide value beyond expectation to our clients. That's our focus. It's providing the services that a client needs, not what we think they need. It's understanding what their needs are. Also, specifically, do they need the whole package or do they need just part of it? That's a success in itself. That we give them a little bit, and we also teach them.

How do I teach people that event planning doesn't need to be the fifth most stressful job, according to *Forbes* magazine two years in a row? That's not a badge of honor. I've created this six-step process to create a simple event-management success system. I'm building it out. It's methodical. If I do events, plan events, and execute, and post about events in a systematic way, it's not stressful, but I've got to take those steps. It's just like Alcoholics Anonymous; there are steps. Everything has a method. That's something that I'm passionate about right now.

For example, hotel contracts are complicated. What happens is that businesses give admins the job to negotiate a hotel contract, sign a contract, and they don't know what they're signing. A lot of the times, I get the aftermath where they're in financial liability because the person that was signing that contract didn't understand what they were signing. So one of the things that we're doing now is building guidelines on how to read a hotel contract. My passion is teaching now. I still have all the event planning and conferences and all of that, but I like this part of it.

I do plan on writing my book. The mastermind I belong to is incredible. They are all coaches, and serial entrepreneurs, so interacting with them is so much fun. One of the things they want me to do is write a book and it could become my speaking platform. I know there's a method to that too.

KEVAN HALL

CEO, Global Integration

www.global-integration.com

I have some core habits, but I'm also appalled by routine.

One book I always recommend to people is *Leadership and Self-Deception*. It takes a metaphor of a couple having various arguments about things and then applies it to the broader society. The story of that is that everyone is a hero in his or her own story and everyone reinterprets the world to make them the good guy or the good girl. It's a wise book and getting into the habit of thinking what the world looks like from the other person's point of view makes things a lot easier. It researches arbitration in international wars and is quite a profound book.

Another book I like is *Rich Dad Poor Dad*, which is good for anyone who is making their way in the world, breaking out of the hamster wheel of making more money and spending more money. It presents a sensible way to organize our lives.

I read many business books, and the counterpoint to that is science fiction. I'm either reading business books or science fiction. One of the books I've enjoyed reading most was *The Martian*. There's so much we can learn from science fiction about human nature and the human capacity for creativity and imagination. It's a beautiful thing.

I've written three books myself which are available through Amazon and other online stores. *Speed Lead*, published in

2006, is my first book about faster, simpler ways to manage people, projects and teams in complex companies. It serves as a practical guide to virtual and matrix working. It's about how to get things done quickly in complex organizations.

Making the Matrix Work, published in 2013, is my second book about how matrix managers create engagement and cut through complexity. In this complex environment in which there are multiple bosses and accountability without control, how do we engage people and cut through complexity?

The most recent one, which came out in 2018, is called *Kill Bad Meetings.* It's about how to improve collaboration by cutting out 50 percent of our meetings. Many people, when they look at meetings, focus on giving people the skills to run better meetings. We do that but not until we've looked at whether that meeting needs to happen in the first place. Otherwise, we're just giving people the skills to run unnecessary meetings.

We've developed an excellent methodology in the book where we go through and sit in and analyze meetings, and people can do it themselves using the tools there and appreciate that 40 percent of the stuff that gets discussed doesn't need to be addressed collectively. Between 10 and 15 percent of the people shouldn't even be in the room.

Why are we even having this meeting? Before we get into the question of how to make it better, can we ask whether it's even important? Many times, when we're working in a team setting, nobody likes that guy who's sitting in the corner saying, "Why are we even doing this?" They want to get on with it. They don't want to think about why they're doing what they're doing.

Well, that leads to another one of the themes that goes through the whole of my work, which is that teamwork is overrated. We've been on a journey on which teamwork has been the answer to everything. As a consequence we're all on multiple teams, we're all in too many meetings. We can't get a decision made because everyone is involved.

Part of the work that we do is getting people to think a lot more mindfully about who needs to be involved in this or that. Is a team the best way to get it done? Maybe we should empower individuals and let them do their job rather than have them report back to a committee of idiots. That's an idea that we convey to people every year. It's a revelation to most people to think, "Maybe we're not a team." There are times where we all need to be a team but just as many times where we don't, and realizing that is important.

KEVIN BOURQUIN

Director of Operations, Cyber Graphics

www.cybermemphis.com

I believe being well-read and well-versed in a variety of topics helps carry on those conversations and develop those relationships that are important in leaders.

Growing up in Baltimore in the North and now working in the South, some of the things I see that Northerners have that may not be as important to the South have helped me. My parents ingrained education in me, so the reading and teaching of all of those habits have been instilled in me from a young age. They set a groundwork for me upon which I could build other habits or strategies that have set me up for success.

One of the most significant habits that I've had to refine is communication. I was a shy introvert growing up and in my career role that wasn't an option. I had to develop strategies to feel more comfortable in those situations and to understand the person I was talking to and how I needed to come across. Adjusting my communication has been influential in my career, and I've had a chance to learn from many great salespeople and technical presenters that have influenced me in how I approach others.

The World is Flat by Thomas L. Friedman has been an influential book for me. It helped me to open up my thinking from a narrow-minded track and understand how outside influences are influencing what we're doing and how we need to influence in return.

Malcolm Gladwell's *The Outliers* is a great book for looking at how data and certain items set themselves apart. Another book I've enjoyed is called *Scenario*. It explains scenario planning and looking at a situation and trying to identify internal and external influences that can change. It's about how to figure out how to think about that ahead of time and plan for them and develop a model or Plan A or Plan B.

That's been helpful for me as we look at different technologies and how we would handle new customers, and what could potentially go wrong. It's helped me to be more prepared and not put myself in a situation where I have to think on my feet and potentially make a bad decision.

Right now, I'm reading *Measure What Matters*. It's about how data is influencing a lot more of what we do. We can spend a whole lot of time collecting all this data — which takes time and costs money — but how do we properly understand the data that we're getting? It's a vital indicator of the result we're going to get and making sure we're efficient with data. We have access to so much of it now that we're connected in the digital world. With too much data, we can't make sense of it. With too little data, we're not given the complete answer. Understanding the best data is an essential skill set for me.

Two main actions make great leaders — the ability to build relationships and the ability to manage change. The only way to do that is to be able to communicate. To communicate properly, I've got to be able to think strategically ahead of what's going on and know how I'm going to react to different situations. Then I make it personal with people and understand what drives them, what motivates them, and let them be part of the process. Those are two things that I have built my entire career on.

If I were to write a book, that would be my topic. Developing communication skills is fundamental, especially nowadays. When we're writing a book for the younger generation, who get to hide behind technology, and when we see these millennials enter the business environment, they're not as comfortable when we're challenging them one on one. We're giving them critical feedback that they need to respond to right away. It's a skill that's hard to teach. We need a lot of practice and coaching and video rehearsal. I gave a talk about that last week, and I will be chairing a conference next week in Cleveland that has a topic around generational leadership.

I have seen in my career clients who conduct their entire business via text message. There's never any face-to-face communication, and I don't understand how their business survives in that manner. It's all open to interpretation on the other end. It's the same with emails, but especially text messages.

It helps to be able to control how a message is received, and the more personal it becomes, the more we have a chance to read body language and look someone in the eye versus reading words on a device. As punctuation becomes less important, we can't control how that message is received. We can't control how someone puts a voice to that message, and it may not be how we intended it to come across. We're so concerned about getting a record of what happened rather than having a more meaningful conversation. Conversation is becoming a lost art.

CONCLUSION

There you have it!

In our year-long interview process with more than 70 supreme leaders, we noticed definitive trends amongst their daily habits. It's evident that the more you resonate with and develop supreme leadership habits, the higher your chances are of being a successful entrepreneur.

Every day — whether you are aware of it or not — your habits, secrets, philosophies, rituals and routines are paving the way toward your future. Now that you've read the success stories of our selection of leaders, you have seen the evidence how these successful entrepreneurs have developed habits that played a role in their success.

Throughout the interview process with these impressive folks, the frank discussions about how habits can be initially developed, learned and significantly honed inspired us. We were impressed by how the leaders were able to turn their perceived shortcomings into strengths. Now there's no excuse not to get out there and make it happen for yourself!

The habits these leaders have developed have enabled and assisted them in running their companies for a quarter of a century each. We all know that their success didn't come overnight — and it didn't come without daily rituals.

Some of these leaders were born with an entrepreneurial spirit. Others pay great attention to their relationships with those around them, including clients, customers, family, neighbors and local communities. A great many of our leaders emphasized their natural-born positive habits. Still others used their negative habits, such as multitasking, to their benefit. Morning routines were specifically beneficial to our leaders, including exercise, spirituality, organization and time spent with family, with pets or in nature. Lastly, our leaders read a lot — books, articles, newsfeeds and more traditional news media.

What do some of our leaders do with these years of accumulated expertise and knowledge? Write a book, of course!

We're sure you'll agree that wherever you are in your career, you have found some inspiration for your future. Whether you are just starting your entrepreneurial career, looking for a kick-start, or just cruising along and hoping to pick up some advice from seasoned experts, these supreme leaders you met have the advice to help you.

Whether you're an early bird, a night owl, a natural entrepreneur or a reader who learns how to run your business in the best way you can, we trust that you've picked up some essential entrepreneurial tips. After all, you've just read advice accumulated by leaders with a total of almost 2,000 years in business!

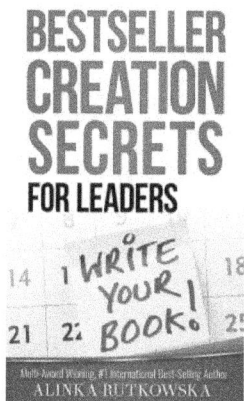

ACKNOWLEDGEMENTS

This book would not have been possible without the passion and dedication of my team at Leaders Press.

Special thanks go to Deborah Brannon and Jill Cotterman. They collectively interviewed dozens of CEOs, creating a professional and friendly atmosphere, and asking insightful questions that allowed us to discover the exact habits that entrepreneurs can replicate to achieve success.

My warmest appreciation goes to Marlayna Glynn, our chief writer, who put this book together and whose writing we're able to launch on top of the bestseller charts with a 100 percent hit rate.

Thank you to our copy editor, Andrew Whiteside, who not only diligently checks every book we release but also creates our press releases and numerous articles.

Finally, I'm truly grateful to our team working behind the scenes scouting for reviewers, getting our books into libraries, licensing rights to foreign publishers, driving publicity, and doing everything that needs to be done to make each of our releases a #1 bestseller.

ABOUT THE AUTHOR

Alinka Rutkowska is a *USA Today* bestselling author, a *Wall Street Journal* bestselling author and an Amazon Top 100 bestselling author in business and money. She's sold more than 100,000 copies of her books. Her approach to book creation has been showcased in *Entrepreneur* magazine.

She's the CEO of Leaders Press and has launched all its titles to bestseller status. She founded LibraryBub, which connects independent authors with 10,000+ librarians.

As a lecturer, she's much sought after and has been voted a Top 5 speaker and named most creative book marketer at the Bestseller Summit Online.

She's been featured on ABC, NBC, CBS, Fox Business, Writer's Digest, Alliance of Independence Authors, International Book Publishers' Association and many more.

To chat with Alinka or one of our book advisors about turning your book idea into a bestseller, go to www.outsourcemybook.com.

www.ingramcontent.com/pod-product-compliance
Lightning Source LLC
Chambersburg PA
CBHW020159200326
41521CB00005BA/186

* 9 7 8 1 9 4 3 3 8 6 3 4 5 *